Suboxone

Take Back Your Life From Pain Medications

D0942937

by

James Schaller, M.D., M.A.R.

Cover Design by Philip Chow

Book Production by Ronald Gombach

Hope Academic Press
Tampa, Florida

ISBN 0-9772729-0-7

Are You Ready to Get Your Life Back?

To David Pilch and Mike Delaney for years of loving service to thousands in New York State.

And to Doug Schoeninger, David Behar, Ralph Eckerdt, Thomas Whiteman and Brian Connor for long-term friendship.

Acknowledgements

My sincere thanks to Michael Sheehan, a leading addiction psychiatrist in Tampa for fifty lessons, and to Scott Kreifels for being an exceptionally passionate and careful editor.

Contents

Contents

Contents

Contents

Finally, an amazing medication exists to enable you to come off of legal and illegal opioid medications in a short time with no discomfort. I really do mean "no discomfort" if prescribed with close contact with your physician in the first few days.

The support for Suboxone is so strong, that government agencies that agree on little, agree on the benefit of Suboxone. Agencies and medical groups who fight over chronic pain treatments, melt into cozy intimacy when the topic is changed to Suboxone. Why?

* 3% of Americans use pain relievers in non-medical ways. Suboxone can remove their physical dependence in 1-3 days.

* You can be detoxed from Oxycontin, oxycodone, Percocet, Dilaudid, Vicodin, hydroxymorphine, codeine and even modest doses of Methadone at your own pace.

* If you stop your Suboxone the withdrawal is mild compared to regular opioids.

* Suboxone is prescribed privately in a physician's office.

* If you have mild-significant pain, Suboxone may be successful in controlling the pain.

* If your pain is cured, you can terminate Suboxone quite rapidly with no distress.

* Suboxone can be called in to your local pharmacy over the phone.

* Suboxone removes all narcotic cravings.

* It does not cause euphoria or a "high" with sublingual use, so it is rarely abused. It can offer a mild contented feeling.

* Suboxone has an anti-abuse drug mixed in to prevent IV use.

* The current abusers of controlled substances come from all walks of life. Suboxone fits everyone's life style.

* If you slip and use your old narcotic, it will not work.

* You stay alert on Suboxone and do not appear drunk.

* Suboxone has a good safety record.

* You can rapidly return to work or school. No rehabilitation center—None.

* No stigma. People who would never consider a daily methadone center love Suboxone.

* Rapid relief of withdrawal symptoms in 15-45 minutes because it is rapidly absorbed into the blood stream under the tongue.

* The dose that works is the dose you stay on. No increased dosing needed.

* Not popular as a "street" drug.

* Taken in the privacy or your own home or office.

* You get your life back!

Real World People and Suboxone

Jamie grew up with excellent grades and had a loving family. She did not use drugs as a youth. She graduated at the top of her class in college and loved her job. Jamie became addicted to Percocet and Vicodin after multiple surgeries. She got her Percocet by seeing multiple doctors and ordering them off the Internet.

Then Jamie accidentally became pregnant—she had the impression that was impossible because of her severe endometriosis. She panicked. She tried to quit her opioids, but relapsed weekly. Her family was annoyed and beyond fed up. Her family had an intervention and she went to an in-patient rehab for a month. After a brief time she relapsed. Her husband separated from her. Then she was placed on Suboxone, and she was stunned at the exciting result. She lost her mild monthly endometriosis ache. Jamie also lost her lust for pain medications—**in one day.** She has been doing well for some time, and has her family and husband back.

*****

David Alexander, 56, struggled with addiction to painkillers for much of his life until he found success with a new drug called buprenorphine [Suboxone] ... After years of battling an addiction to painkillers ... for numerous injuries he suffered while racing motorcycles, Alexander no longer craves the narcotics.

His salvation is ... buprenorphine. "It saved my life," says Alexander, ... who has been taking "bupe" ... 3 1/2 years ago. "And I'm not being dramatic." [1]

*****

Michelle had a surgery last year and was placed on Percocet. They removed her significant pain, but they also made her feel "good." She was not used to feeling this good. After her physician stopped renewing her prescription, she bought Percocets and Fentanyl and similar medications illegally. She loved the way she felt, but feared being caught. When she reduced her dose she had withdrawal symptoms. She was also afraid of hurting her liver—more than thirteen Percocets per day could cause liver injury. She was stabilized on Suboxone in two days. Then she weaned off the Suboxone over seven weeks. She is doing fine, and has found many fun things in her life to enjoy to replace her addiction.

*****

Tom has suffered with the effects of joint pain for over ten years. He had Lyme disease that went undiagnosed for a decade and dissolved some cartilage. He took Oxycontin for pain. While it was fully effective, he disliked the looks the pharmacist would give him and the devaluating comments from relatives, who called him an "addict." He said, "I would like to stick I nail in their joints and see how long it takes them to start using pain medications."

But finally, he was tired of all the KGB pain monitoring when he lost a 1/4 bottle of Oxycontin in a camping trip. His physician asked him to complete a police report and reduced his dose. "As if punishment for being a bad boy," he said.

So Tom decided to convert to Suboxone in a day, and started using a special narcotic compounded cream that went right into his knee joints through the skin, but not through his entire body. He found the pain cream reduced his knee pain 80% and Suboxone 8 mg every eight hours removed the rest of his pain.

*****

John and Lisa attended a methadone clinic for two years. It was the center of their life. Each day they went to the methadone center to get their dose. Each passing season they said they were treated with less respect and dignity. They had been addicted to heroin. They tried to reduce their dosage of methadone in very tiny amounts, and yet they felt ill and uncomfortable with even minimal withdrawals. **They were switched from methadone to Suboxone in three days,** and now both enjoy working and meeting new friends outside the methadone clinic. After trying out a number of different jobs, each loves their work and the "regular people" who are their new friends.

Doctor's Love the Results

Doctors who prescribe buprenorphine say the reward is great.

"There are just not that many things you do that so dramatically change peoples' lives," says ... [Dr.] Sullivan ... "They recoup their lives, their families, their jobs, their self-esteem." [2]

*****

Dr. Richard Campana became interested in Suboxone when his friend did research on the medication. ... The results of her study with Suboxone were "nothing short of astounding." So Campana took a Suboxone training program. He liked that Suboxone could be prescribed by a doctor in the office, and did not require the patient to return daily. Patients are free to live a normal life, and feel "normal but not high."

The withdrawal from Suboxone is less intense than other opioids, and people can be successfully weaned from Suboxone. Opioid dependence, according to Dr. Campana, spares no sector of the population and can be found in all ethnic groups, socioeconomic classes, and anyone predisposed to chemical addictions. "I treat individuals ranging from high-profile business owners to teachers, professionals, housewives, and high school students." This physician talks of three individuals with opioid addiction..." They were all very intelligent and from solid, loving families. Yet each of them was being consumed by ... addiction. Their families were devastated.

"I am happy to say that once these young men started taking Suboxone, their withdrawal symptoms and drug cravings completely dissipated and their general sense of well-being improved dramatically. All of their follow-up drug screens have been negative. They are all gainfully employed or working on advanced educational degrees."

Reflecting on his work, Campana said, "My satisfaction comes from knowing that these young men, who are not much older than my own son, now have a real chance to get on with their lives and become productive citizens in this community." [3]

Suboxone is Often Superior
to Other Maintenance or Detox Options

Methadone
Methadone replaces fast acting street opioids. Compared to other legal and illegal opioids, Methadone lasts longer, has less euphoria and prevents opioid withdrawal symptoms. But you must go to the clinic almost daily, it is very hard to detox from heroin and it is very deadly in overdose or an accidental poisoning of a child. (However, if you have very severe opioid cravings that **truly** require **very high** methadone levels, it is useful).

LAAM
LAAM was approved to treat opioid addiction in the USA, but its maker stopped distribution in 2003, mainly because of reports of severe heart-related side effects.

Rapid Detox with Anesthesia
On the surface this treatment looks appealing. You are put to sleep while you go through a rapid opioid withdrawal. But anesthesia-assisted opioid withdrawal has a risk for life-threatening adverse events. In one study the anesthesia-assisted protocol gave 1/12 patients serious adverse events. This treatment costs $10,000 to $15,000 and is not covered by health insurance. A patient is put asleep while two very strong anti-opioids are administered. Finally, the outcomes are poor for this method since many patients relapse. [4-7] In contrast, Suboxone can be continued for months or years to prevent opioid cravings.

Anti-Opioid Medications
Medications like naloxone and naltrexone block opioids and make any opioid abused ineffective. So if a person relapsed, the opioid would not work. If a patient was already on regular opioids and these were added, the person would experience severe and profound withdrawal immediately, with severe diarrhea, nausea, vomiting. This abrupt immediate detox can be life threatening.

Physicians do prescribe oral naltrexone **after** a person is finished a detoxification to help prevent relapses, since no opioid is effective while on it. But few patients like this approach. [8]

Symptom Relief Detox Medications
Some physicians use Catapress (clonidine) to reduce opioid withdrawal symptoms but it does not treat all of the symptoms of severe withdrawal. [9] Additional medications are added such as Phenergan or Compazine for nausea, Imodium or Kaopectate for diarrhea, or muscle relaxants like Flexeril, Skelaxin or Robaxin for severe muscle pain. However, muscle relaxants can cause drowsiness and also have a risk of seizures, especially in patients having some alcohol or benzodiazepine withdrawal. Some physicians also occasionally add anti-anxiety agents like Ativan, Valium, Klonopin and Serax. But none of these medications are effective maintenance treatments to prevent future opioid cravings.

Suboxone is Not New

Generally, the United States approves medications years or even decades after other advanced countries. In a country that opposes health claims of essential nutrients, this should be no surprise. For example the active ingredient of Suboxone, buprenorphine, was in use in the United Kingdom over a quarter of a century ago. In 1975, Cowan and Lewis were crouching behind one-way mirrors to see if it had any effect on monkeys. [10] The effect was obvious and profound. The following results in humans were so compelling that the United Kingdom approved it in a shot or injection form in 1978 and then a sublingual (under the tongue) form in 1981. [11]

The most extensive treatment experience with buprenorphine is in France, where it has been routinely used since 1996. In France, it is prescribed to about 70,000 patients.

Buprenorphine studies have used 1 mg to 32 mg. The studies show buprenorphine has excellent results—reduced opioid abuse, patients generally stay in treatment, limited side effects and most patients like it.

Opioid Problems: Poorly Treated in the Past

Methadone was first used in the 1960s and it offered a safe and effective treatment to prevent heroin use. Suddenly people with opioid addiction were working and taking care or their children and improving their lives. Then a flood of laws made getting methadone as hard to get as uranium. Laws in 1972 and 1974, limited methadone treatment to highly regulated methadone clinics that required almost daily attendance. So basically no one could work and contribute to society who needed methadone for serious opioid cravings.

Soon the stigma of these clinics and the **massive inconvenience** made it so over 75% of people with an opioid addiction did not receive treatment (according to the National Institutes of Health, 1997). Further, since few physicians work in these methadone centers, few were up to date with opioid problems.

The FDA approved Suboxone in the USA in 2002

In 2000, a law called "the Drug Addiction Treatment Act of 2000" allowed "certified" physicians to be able to bypass the methadone-type rules. And then in 2002 the FDA approved two new sublingual formulations for opioid addiction—Subutex (buprenorphine) and Suboxone (buprenorphine/naloxone).

To use these medications physicians complete at least 8 hours of special training in opioid addiction or have other special addiction certifications, e.g., a certification in addiction medicine. Now a doctor can treat addiction to opioids in their office. But obviously treating your dependence is not as simple as an excellent medication (Suboxone). Therefore this new law requests that a **full treatment plan** be offered beyond just Suboxone. We will discuss these options later. Yet I have never found them to be a major burden, and I have never had anyone reject Suboxone because I tried to take over their limited free time. You work with your doctor to try to grow a little each month in preventing relapse and improving your health.

Addiction: The Bottom Line

Opioid addiction is when a person repeatedly and compulsively seeks to use an opioid despite significant consequences to their relationships, emotional health and/or physical health.

Sometimes addiction has physical dependence, withdrawal feelings, and tolerance. Physical dependence is clearly present if you stop the drug and you have symptoms and signs of withdrawal. *Opioid Withdrawal* is a set list of body and emotional signs and symptoms that occur when you abruptly stop a medication, e.g., nausea, sweating and irritability. *Tolerance* is when you need higher doses to have the same initial effect.

It is possible to be physically dependent on a drug without being addicted. For example, chronic pain patients with cancer or severe arthritis are dependent on opioid pain medications and also have tolerance and physical dependence. But they are not addicted.

Suboxone Helps Reduce Big Problems

Currently, there are many types of opioids available to become dependent on. These include Oxycontin, Percocet, Dilaudid, methadone, oxycodone, and heroin. The latter, heroin, may have one million people who are addicted. This addiction increases crime, unemployment, illness and death. Current heroin is very potent and pure, and can cause a high just with snorting or smoking. Some switch to injecting as they get tolerant or if the purity falls, which increases HIV, along with hepatitis B and C infections. Addiction in general leads to danger with high risk driving, impulsive sexual behavior and poor preventive medical and dental care. In 2003, more than 200,000 individuals in the United States were maintained on long acting methadone or an equivalent.

Suboxone Reduces the Demand for Opioids for Abuse

I am confident that a Suboxone user represents one less person abusing illegal opioids. They become individuals who do not have to fear arrest.

The Real Sources of Pain Medicine Abuse

Many media and government officials are utterly clueless about the source of abused opioids. They mistakenly think these prescription opioids are from physicians treating pain. **Yet the DEA reports 90% of diverted street pain medications come from sources *other* than physician prescriptions, e.g., pharmacy theft.** The DEA and Media- addicted district attorneys like to portray pain medicine on the street as coming from physicians, but this is false, and has ended medical pain care and increased suicides due to pain.

Joranson DE, Gilson AM. Drug crime is a source of abused pain medications in the United States. *J Pain Symptom Manage.* 2005; 30:299-301.

Available at:
www.medsch.wisc.edu/painpolicy/publicat/05jpsm/05jpsm.pdf

PDF Version of Press Release at:
www.medsch.wisc.edu/painpolicy/publicat/05jpsm/press_release.pdf.

Use Suboxone or Face Great Risk

The risk of death if someone uses IV heroin is about 10% a year. [12] But other risks include assault, arrest and massive economic losses to purchase your opioid of choice. Here are a few examples:

* Driving into dangerous neighborhoods or interacting with risky people is a risk for assault, theft and arrest.

* "Good friends" routinely turn in their buyers to get a lesser prison sentence.

* Some insanely high prices off the Internet. Prices that can be 10-20x the cost of Suboxone. Over time this drains your bank account.

Suboxone's Good Feelings Offer a Hopeful Alternative

In our experience buprenorphine can produce contentment. It has even been found to help depression. [13]

Some medical studies and French drug addicts (who abused it for a short time) report buprenorphine can also produce mild euphoria, but less than regular opioids, especially if it is injected. Suboxone will cause a profound withdrawal if injected due to the presence of naloxone—a complete **opioid blocker.** Since naloxone is approximately 15 times more potent by injection than by the sublingual Suboxone route, if it is injected the naloxone should cause a severe withdrawal.

Suboxone also produces a physical dependence, but it is much less than any other regular opioid like heroin, oxycodone, or methadone. It also is easier to discontinue at the end of treatment—compared to other full pain medications or other opioids like heroin, methadone or oxycodone.

Dosage Forms of Buprenorphine in the United States [14]

Medication	Trade Name	Dosage Form(s)	Indication	Company	FDA-Approved for Opioid Addiction Treatment
Buprenor-phine	Subutex	2 - or 8 -mg sublingual tablets	Opioid ad-diction	Reckitt Benckiser	Yes
Buprenor-phine/ naloxone combina-tion	Suboxone	2 - or 8 -mg sublingual tablets with buprenor-phine/ naloxone in 4:1 ratio	Opioid ad-diction	Reckitt Benckiser	Yes
Buprenor-phine	Buprenex	Injectable ampules	Moderate - to -severe pain	Reckitt Benckiser	No
Buprenor-phine	Buprenor-phine injectable (generic)	Injectable ampules	Moderate - to -severe pain	Abbott Laboratories	No

SUBOXONE is shown below in the 2 mg and 8 mg strengths.

2 mg buprenorphine + 0.5 mg naloxone

8 mg buprenorphine + 2 mg naloxone [15]

Suboxone Basics

Again, Suboxone is a combination medication made up of a buprenorphine and naloxone. (The naloxone is added so if someone were crazy enough to inject Suboxone IV, it would prevent an overdose or a high). But the real medication in Suboxone is a highly unusual opioid called "buprenorphine" which is also nicknamed "bupe." It is very unique in that it is able to stimulate the opioid receptors **partly,** and it also blocks pain receptors partly.

Buprenorphine was first sold as a pain medicine. But now its use is mainly for treating opioid addiction.

Buprenorphine is an example of a partial stimulator (agonist) of the pain receptor mu. The figure below shows the pain receptor mu stimulated fully by methadone, partially stimulated by buprenorphene and blocked fully by naloxone.

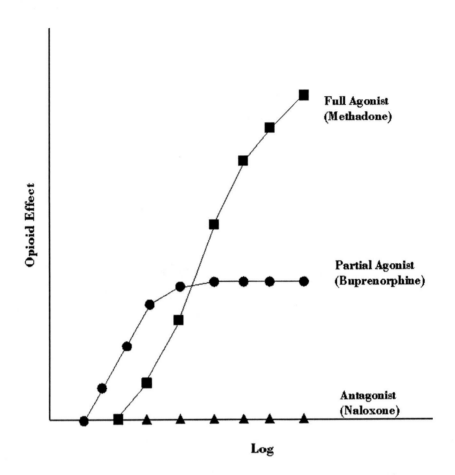

* This graph is not for dosing purposes. [16]

Forms of Suboxone

The forms of buprenorphine currently available in the USA are **Subutex** and **Suboxone**. (An injectable form of buprenorphine is FDA approved for pain and called, "Buprenex," but it has no use in opioid addiction).

Subutex is a lemon-lime sublingual tablet in 2mg and 8mg forms. It is a simpler medication and has no naloxone, so some physicians use this for the first few days of treatment when a person might have long acting narcotics like methadone in their system. Suboxone is an orange flavored sublingual in 2mg and 8 mg hexagon shaped tablets. It has one part naloxone for every four parts buprenorphine. Naloxone blocks opioids from working and routinely saves lives in emergency rooms when people take acutely high overdoses of pain medications or heroin.

Why is Suboxone Sublingual?

Some forget to take their medication this way, so it is worth an explanation. Most medications are not sublingual. So why is this medication in this unusual form? Simply, when you swallow a pill, it is absorbed from the gut and cleaned-up by the liver. In the case of buprenorphine, the "first pass" or the first time the liver "cleans" it from the blood is quite effective and drops the useful dose too low to be useful. Indeed, if you swallow Suboxone you lose 80% of its effectiveness.

Suboxone Safety

In contrast to most medications, Suboxone probably has limited increased effects over 32 mg. This is a protective feature. So if a small toddler accidentally ingests it, they would probably survive. If that same child swallowed methadone or high dose oxycodone pills, they would probably die.

Suboxone usually does not impair thinking or alertness, so you have less risk of sedation problems. This means less DUI driving and less chance you will appear impaired to neighbors, friends, children, spouses or employers. In contrast to methadone "nodding" and occasional sedation, I have yet to see a Suboxone patient look "stoned."

Further, other than occasional increases in liver enzymes (usually in liver diseased patients) buprenorphine seems to be very safe to the human body.

Practical Suboxone Treatment

Suboxone treatment has some very unique procedures. It is not like seeing your family doctor, getting a diagnosis of a raw "strept throat," and filling an antibiotic at your pharmacy. Below are sample things you may experience with Suboxone treatment. Please be aware not all physicians follow this pattern exactly. Many very smart and experienced physicians have other procedures.

Setting Up Treatment

Most offices have a fee schedule and a procedure for your transition from an opioid like Percocet, Dilaudid or Oxycontin to Suboxone. If you are sent materials, please read them. My experience is that most patients make errors in the first 2 days of treatment. Most can be prevented by reading all intake educational materials and following directions.

Typically, we suggest that no opioid be taken 24 hours before your intake appointment. This way most opioids will be out of your system and you can start Suboxone immediately. (If you are converting from methadone, you will probably need other directions, including waiting to start Suboxone **at least two days** after your last dose).

I *strongly suggest* **that you start Suboxone only after the beginning of** *mild-moderate* **withdrawal symptoms.** If you "slip" and use a narcotic just before your appointment with your physician, please tell him or her. Since you are struggling with opioid dependence, it is not a catastrophe. However, if you add Suboxone a few hours after taking an opioid like Percocet, oxycodone, Oxycontin or heroin, you will have a significant withdrawal reaction. If you take long acting methadone and then start Suboxone the same day, you will also have a strong withdrawal "precipitated" by Suboxone. So you must have some mild withdrawal symptoms before you start Suboxone.

Never Start Suboxone or Subutex "High"

Buprenorphine has the ability to cause withdrawal if other opioids are present in your body. **So Suboxone should only be started when sufficient time has passed for other opioids to be removed from the body.** The reason is that Buprenorphine binds to pain receptors so strongly that it tosses off other opioids. So if you have just taken Oxycontin, oxycodone, Percocet, Vicodin, Dilaudid, heroin, methadone or other narcotic pain medications, they will be removed from your pain receptors. Therefore, it is possible for buprenorphine to cause a profound and uncomfortable immediate withdrawal.

Sample Signs and Symptoms of Opioid Withdrawal

If a key requirement of Suboxone use is a smart awareness of the various signs and symptoms of opioid withdrawal and the symptoms at each level, it is critical for us to have materials that allow clear communication between a patient and their physician. You do not want to think you are in severe withdrawal, when you have barely any withdrawal symptoms. But you do not want to wait until you have severe withdrawal, since that is merely suffering for no real purpose.

Levels of Opioid Withdrawal [17]

Stage	Grade	Physical Signs/Symptoms
Early Withdrawal (8–24 hours after last use)	Grade 1	Tearing Runny nose Sweating Yawning Restlessness Insomnia
	Grade 2	Dilated pupils Muscle twitching Muscle aches Joint aches Abdominal pain Hair "stands on end" or goose-bumps
Fully Developed Withdrawal (1–3 days after last use)	Grade 3	Rapid pulse High blood pressure Rapid breathing Fever Disinterest in food Nausea Extreme restlessness
	Grade 4	Diarrhea Vomiting Dehydration High blood sugar Hypotension Curled-up position

Clinical Opiate Withdrawal Scale (COWS) [18]

For each item below, circle the number that best describes the patient's signs or symptoms. Generally, rate just what applies to opiate withdrawal. For example, if a heart rate were increased because the patient was jogging just prior to assessment, the increased pulse rate would not add to the score.

Patient Name:	Date:	Time:

Reason for this assessment:

1. Resting pulse rate: _____ beats/minute Measured after the patient is sitting or lying for one minute.
0 Pulse rate 80 or below
1 Pulse rate 81-100
2 Pulse rate 101-120
4 Pulse rate greater than 120

2. Sweating: over past half hour not accounted for by room temperature or patient activity
0 No reports of chills or flushing
1 Subjective reports of chills or flushing
2 Flushed or observable moisture on face
3 Beads of sweat on brow or face
4 Sweat streaming off face

3. Restlessness: observation during assessment
0 Able to sit still
1 Reports difficulty sitting still, but is able to do so
3 Frequent shifting or extraneous movements of legs/arms
5 Unable to sit still for more than a few seconds

4. Pupil size
0 Pupils pinned or normal size for room light
1 Pupils possibly larger than normal for room light
2 Pupils moderately dilated
5 Pupils so dilated that only the rim of the iris is visible

5. **Bone or joint aches:** if patient was having pain previously, only the additional component attributed to opiate withdrawal is scored.
0 Not present
1 Mild diffuse discomfort
2 Patient reports severe diffuse aching of joints/muscles
4 Patient is rubbing joints or muscles and is unable to sit still because of discomfort

6. **Runny nose or tearing:** not accounted for by cold symptoms or allergies
0 Not present
1 Nasal stuffiness or unusually moist eyes
2 Nose running or tearing
4 Nose constantly running or tears streaming down cheeks

7. **GI upset:** over last half hour
0 No GI symptoms
1 Stomach cramps
2 Nausea or loose stool
3 Vomiting or diarrhea
5 Multiple episodes of diarrhea or vomiting

8. **Tremor:** observation of outstretched hands
0 No tremor
1 Tremor can be felt, but not observed
2 Slight tremor observable
4 Gross tremor or muscle twitching

9. **Yawning:** observation during assessment
0 No yawning
1 Yawning once or twice during assessment
2 Yawning three or more times during assessment
4 Yawning several times/minute

10. Anxiety or irritability
0 None
1 Patient reports increasing irritability or anxiousness
2 Patient obviously irritable, anxious
4 Patient so irritable or anxious that participation in the assessment is difficult

11. Gooseflesh skin
0 Skin is smooth
3 Piloerection of skin can be felt or hairs standing up on arms
5 Prominent piloerection

Total Score: _____

[The total score is the sum of all 11 items.] Initials of person completing assessment: _____

Score:
   5–12=Mild;
   13–24=Moderate;
   25–36=Moderately severe;
   >36=Severe withdrawal

If you like this scale you can find a PDF formatted version of the COWS from the websites of the American Society of Addiction Medicine, the California Society of Addiction Medicine, the UCLA Integrated Substance Abuse Programs, and AlcoholMD.com.

A Simple Opioid Withdrawal Signs and Symptoms Scale [19]

(0 is none and 5 is severe)

*Headache   _____

*Constipation   _____

*Diarrhea   _____

*Sweating   _____

*Nausea   _____

*Vomiting   _____

*Uncomfortable mood   _____

*Hair standing on end   _____

*Muscle discomfort   _____

*A runny nose   _____

*Dilated pupils   _____

*Tearing   _____

*Irritability   _____

*Anxiety   _____

*A low-grade fever   _____

*Fantasies of the opioid drug _____

*Yawning   _____

*Trouble sleeping   _____

*Yawning   _____

*Muscle twitching   _____

*Restless   _____

The Simplest Alcohol and Drug Screen Questions

A busy family doctor or internist might only have a couple minutes to explore your vulnerability to alcohol or drugs. Look over these questions honestly, and see if any of the four applies to you.

CAGE - AID: The CAGE Questions Adapted To Include Drugs [20]

The goal of this scale is not to fully document opioid or other substance addiction, but to allow you to calmly, and without any reactive defensiveness, ponder your use of opioids and other drugs or alcohol. It is a short and to the point reflection tool, not an accusation. Here are the four CAGE-AID questions:

* Have you felt you ought to **C**ut down on your drinking or drug use?
* Have people **A**nnoyed you by criticizing your drinking or drug use?
* Have you felt bad or **G**uilty about your drinking or drug use?
* Have you ever had a drink or used drugs first thing in the morning to steady your nerves or to get rid of a hangover (**E**ye -opener)?

One or more "yes" responses constitute a positive screening test. Note, however, that due to language barriers, individual interpretation of the questions, or other confounding factors, individuals answering "no" to all CAGE -AID questions may still be at risk due to elevated drinking or drug use.

Using Signs and Symptoms of Withdrawal
To Pick Your Suboxone Dose

You want at least mild opioid withdrawal present **before** you start
Suboxone. If none are present, it may mean your last dose of opioid is
still sitting on the pain receptors. You want them to be largely gone
from the body before you add Suboxone.

Why? Withdrawal signs mean your opioid of choice is gone from the
receptors, and now the buprenorphine can bind to them. If you sneak
one of your legal or illegal opioids the morning of your intake, such as
Oxycontin, percocet, methadone or heroin, and then you take Suboxone immediately—you can actually experience strong withdrawal
symptoms. This is due to the powerful ability of buprenorphine to
displace other opioids—then you will be withdrawing in minutes. But
you certainly do **not** have to wait to start your Suboxone until you
are in agony, since you might impulsively act out and use some other
opioid.

Further, having mild withdrawal symptoms as you are starting Suboxone will be useful in picking the dose that is uniquely best for you.
If your mold withdrawal symptoms go away 100%, you are taking a
useful dose. If some withdrawal symptoms start to break through
during the day, you are obviously underdosed, and will need more.
So these mild withdrawal feelings are a tool to find the correct dose.
You only have to experience mild temporary withdrawal symptoms
during day one of Suboxone treatment.

Suboxone is for Opioid Dependence

While Suboxone has years of use as a pain medication, the government and various medical societies are promoting Suboxone for opioid dependence. So you have to be opioid dependent or "addicted" to
have it prescribed, unless you are seeing someone who treats chronic
pain.

Therefore, you should know the "doctor definition" of dependence to speak the same language:

"Dependence" involves using an opioid like Percocet, Vicodin, heroin, or methadone in a manner that causes trouble. It causes trouble in your basic functioning in relationships, work or with the law. These problems with opioids have to have lasted at least a year.

Many experts feel you need a few of these to be dependent:

1. You get withdrawal signs if you stop or decrease the opioid. You "need" to take an opioid to stop withdrawal.

2. It becomes the center of your life. Your schedule is focused on using a drug and locating it.

3. You cannot stop using it.

4. You have to use very high amounts, far above what you ever intended. The opioid dosing "got away" from you.

5. You need profoundly large amounts to get "high" or your routine amount is no longer effective.

6. You know the opioid is hurting you physically or emotionally, but you cannot stop using it.

7. The opioid hurts your work, parenting, friendships, marriage or "significant other" relationships. Your definition of "fun" and "play" becomes using the opioid.

What About Suboxone for Substance Addiction?

Suboxone is also for individuals who are addicted to opioids. You can be addicted and not have dependence. Addiction is the repeated and compulsive seeking or use of an opioid, despite the fact it is causing problems physically, emotionally or socially. While not every person with addictive behaviors is dependent, you can still have Suboxone if merely addicted.

Day One on Suboxone

Generally, it is too difficult to work the day of your first appointment. This is particularly true if you are a driver or need to have significant attention to do a good job. You do not want to have a car accident or appear sedated your first day on Suboxone. Many physicians like to have repeated contact with you the first day... and different physicians give you a different **maximum** amount of Suboxone the first day. Yet most will increase this top amount if you are obviously still having withdrawal signs and symptoms.

After interviewing other practitioners and looking over hundreds of studies, I learned each physician has a slightly different approach in starting day one. For example:

* Some have you come in for an intake and then go to a local pharmacy and pick up a prescription, and then take your initial doses in their office, with intermittent contact with them or their nurse throughout the day. Some request you physically remain in their office most of the first 1-2 days as you are converted to Suboxone.

* Others do an intake, have you pick up your prescription, and then have you call in at various intervals over the next 1-3 days.

* Finally, some do the intake, and give you more control. You might be told to simply start with 2 mg tablets taken every 45 minutes to an hour to stop any cravings. (Some patients actually do well on low doses). Others tell you to start with a 4 mg tablet. Most clinicians seem to prescribe at least 8 mg for the prevention of withdrawal on day one.

I recommend that you have some access to your physician a couple times during day one and at least once during day two. Personally, I like to talk briefly with my patients at least four times on day one and day two, to make sure they are doing well. If they need more time to talk, I offer it.

While few offices or doctor's are able to spend a large amount of time with you if you are shopping Suboxone doctors, most will give you a sense of their "system." You should be able to find a fit. In some areas, you might have to travel hours to reach a certified Suboxone practitioner, but this should not be a problem. I routinely treat individuals who do not live near my office or even in the same state. While this might seem a little complicated, it is generally routine for physicians to switch people to Suboxone with little trouble, as long as you are willing to be seen for a face-to-face intake and be compliant with your intake labs and a reasonable treatment plan. My experience is most Suboxone doctors should be able to help you, even if you have to travel far to see them. You will not be the first.

How Do I Know How Much to Take?

Simply, during day one you determine with your doctor how much you will need to take during day two. So lets say your doctor gives you a prescription for 2 mg tablets, and you take one every hour for 4 hours (8 mg). But you are starting to feel some mild withdrawal feelings six-ten hours after you initial dose of 8 mg. Your doctor will probably tell you to take more, perhaps an additional 2-6 mg when you talk to them. But each patient and doctor is unique, and this book is not a cookbook.

So you talk to your physician and they have you take some additional Suboxone to cover the evening. Now you feel good for the rest of the day.

If you feel a slight withdrawal at bedtime, you will probably be told what to do in terms of dosing. So lets say you took 16 mg by diner time, but feel a little breakthrough, you might be told to take an extra 2-4 mg. However, do not panic. Suboxone sits on the receptors a long time, so you should not have any major withdrawal even if you have to wait until the morning for further dosing or instructions.

Why I Do Not Like "Gradual" Suboxone Replacement

Some articles instruct physicians to never give over 8 mg of Suboxone on day one, and never more than 16 mg on day two. I reject this simplistic cookbook approach. It is also a good way to make some rare patients lose heart and relapse. Having mild withdrawal for a few hours on day one is very different than 1-2 days of mild to moderate withdrawal symptoms. In some studies, a slow gradual transition to an effective full dose of buprenorphine over several days, led to many patients dropping-out of buprenorphine treatment. Having **anyone** dropping out is a disaster! Therefore, patients should have a clinically effective dose that ends all opioid withdrawal symptoms as soon as possible. [21]

Day Two is Simple

To pick your personalized dose for day two, you just add up what you took on day one. If you took 14 mg in day one without signs of excess dosing, you will probably take 16 mg on day two and you will be just fine. Some physicians suggest taking this at the start of the day in one big dose, and others suggest splitting the dose, e.g., 8 mg in the am and 8 mg later in the afternoon. Some feel taking Suboxone twice a day is like repetitious drug abuse, while others split the dose to help any mild body aches you might have from bruised muscles or inflamed joints. By the way, you are now detoxed from whatever opioid you were on. **Congratulations**.

Day Three—All Done

Now you simply evaluate the dose that worked on day two. You might decide after consulting with your physician to tailor the dose. For example, if you are a person with residue pain, e.g., spine pain, you might feel better with a little more in three divided doses. If you felt uncomfortable with a higher dose, you might drop your dose a little. If you are fed up with opioids you can start to slowly wean down. This is called "detox" or detoxification.

If you want to live without any medication, you can wean yourself off the Suboxone with a plan you and your doctor design. Generally, detox is more successful if you take Suboxone *at least* a month. Some do well decreasing 2 mg per day.

If you find that you are having cravings to abuse your previous opioids, during any detox, you should go back on the Suboxone and explore what might be the cause of your cravings—both medical and psychological. (We will discuss this in later sections).

Follow-Up Sessions with Your Doctor

No set Suboxone program exists for determine your exact follow up treatment. Every physician has a different preference. Simply, they want to make sure you know what you are doing and are comfortable. If you have other issues, such as depression or anxiety, you should also discuss having these treated. Please understand if your doctor wants to "watch over you" the first few weeks, they are trying to do a complete job. Smart people make mistakes with this medication, and the legal or illegal substances you have used may have hurt your body. Further, your problem is not simply a Suboxone deficiency. So you will need some direction to achieve a well-rounded recovery from your addiction problem.

Your Local Pharmacy and Suboxone

While the government is supportive of Suboxone, they require extra paperwork from your local pharmacy to carry it. Some are very happy to have your business, and others do not want to deal with the hassle. Some physicians know which pharmacy carries Suboxone and other pharmacies have to order it in. (A rare physician will dispense it from their office). We suggest that you inquire about suggested pharmacies from the physician's office, before you make an appointment, so you do not have any surprises—like going to a pharmacy with your Suboxone prescription and they do not have any in stock.

Lab Testing to Check Health and Drug Use

Many physicians request that you have some basic blood work done to make sure you liver and other organs are healthy. These are basic labs that only require a couple tubes of blood. We prefer a very comprehensive set of lab studies, but if you have to pay for your own labs, you will probably only be able to afford basic lab testing.

Since many people struggling with other opioids also have trouble with other drugs, your physician will want to get a toxicology urine screen. Struggling with another addiction is not rare, but it is something that should be addressed. Some research shows that Suboxone might help other addiction cravings a little, but do not count on this benefit.

So what if you are addicted to other non-opioids. What will your Suboxone doctor do? Different physicians handle other substance abuse issues differently. But many physicians will respect your conversion to Suboxone as a positive step in the right direction, and will not drop you as a patient if you abuse other substances. However, some physicians are very concerned about the use or abuse of illegal or legal drugs, and will want you to treat these co-addictions immediately.

Personally, I am concerned with possible death and arrest.

For example, if you mix Suboxone with alcohol and benzodiazapines like Ativan, Xanax, Klonopin and Valium it is possible you could stop breathing. Certainly this does not always happen, but **no** physician can tell you what is a safe dose of a benzodiazepine with alcohol and Suboxone, so physicians agree taking three respiratory depressants is too risky.

Generally, many Suboxone doctors would also be concerned with excess alcohol and Suboxone. I cannot tell you the definition of "excess" alcohol, so most Suboxone physicians feel you should avoid alcohol entirely. If you "must" drink, you might be one of those individuals who also has an alcohol problem. Discuss this with your physician so you are able to use Suboxone safely.

The other top issue with other non-opioid addictions is your risk of arrest. First, you definitely do not want to tempt fate and buy illegal drugs since it is only a matter of time before you are arrested and enter the degrading and unpleasant criminal legal system. Liberty is a precious thing—you do not want to lose it. Further, some drugs are legal, like alcohol, but can make you vulnerable to hurting others with a car or with eccentric childcare. You do not want to get a DUI or hurt someone because you are intoxicated. Also, you do not want to be casual about any drug that hurts your body such as cocaine or excess alcohol.

We suggest being "real" with your Suboxone physician, since sooner or later they will discover your other addiction(s). It is possible some physicians might be very concerned about one of your addictions. If you are not able or willing to address this addiction, why deal with someone who will not accept your process of recovery? Of course, if a strict physician offers you a challenge to address a second addiction, why not take up the challenge?

Having made these comments, I have found most Suboxone physicians to be **highly motivated to help you heal, live, and have**

your life back. If they are worried about another addiction that might hurt you or get you arrested, you should probably also be concerned.

Types of Urine Testing

Some physicians have urine test kits in their office and these have different levels of sensitivity. Some require stricter chain of custody samples. Over time you will probably be reduced to random samples. Why? Simply, doctors do not like surprises. They want to know which strange drugs are circling around your body. However, I have yet to find patients reporting this testing is a problem.

No Withdrawal, Does Not Mean Cured

One of the pearls from AA is that once an alcoholic stops drinking, they REALLY start to feel things and they are often called "dry drunks." What does this have to do with you and opioid dependence? You will **not be raw with any opioid withdrawal symptoms on Suboxone,** but you will need to learn how to have a life without euphoric drugs as a cushion. You will need to find other ways to have fun and new ways to enjoy life. You will need new ways to cope with disappointments. This will take some time due to slow body changes, emotional changes and the time required for new relationships. Take comfort in knowing tens of millions have walked this path before you.

Therefore, you should be thinking about how you can work with your physician to come up with a "personal growth recovery plan" which is functional. I admit this sounds vague. So what does a "personal growth recovery plan" mean?

First, if you have other addictions, especially illegal or highly unhealthy ones, you might take a look at ways to stay out of jail and remain alive.

Second, many folks put off basic medical self-care. So if you have not had your teeth cleaned or examined in eighteen months, you are due. If you have not had a PAP smear and a pelvic exam, perhaps now is time.

Third, you will need some things to do which provide you satisfaction. Having activities that are either fun or satisfying helps your recovery. However, once you stop an opioid or painkiller, you will **not** suddenly have twenty things you enjoy or find meaningful. You might be bored for a short time. However, soon you will start thinking of things that are curious and people that are appealing. You need to reflect on some possible interests and try them out. Over time, you will find that different activities or different relationships are satisfying. If you feel I am being too general and not offering any examples, you are right. This is because everyone is so different that the activities and relationships that fill the emptiness in your heart, may differ from everyone else I have ever met.

Suboxone For Pain or Opioid Dependence

Currently US law allows one physician to have 30 patients on Suboxone or Subutex for **opioid addiction** at a time. If your doctor is one of the very rare physicians who also provide pain treatment, and you are using Suboxone for pain treatment, then I have been told that these patients do not count in the 30 patients. However, **pain treatment requires *very aggressive proof* you have a pain disorder.** Further, if you abuse illegal narcotics or other addictive substances, you will never be seen as a "pain patient."

The research on this medication is that while it binds the primary pain receptor tightly, it is not the same as stimulation. So practically this means it will help mild to severe pain. But people vary a great deal in their experience with pain relief. We have seen patients with mild muscle and joint aches only get mild relief with Suboxone, and others with severe pain occasionally have complete relief.

So you cannot really know what type of pain relief is possible for a person without a trial. Further, some physicians and agencies do not agree on the degree of pain relief. For example, the Joint Formulary Committee of Australia do not recommend the use of buprenorphine for pain. They do not promote it for pain because it prevents the anti-opioid naloxone from working during a buprenorphine overdose. They also feel it has mild addictive qualities, and if added to other opioids—combinations of opioids are used with some chronic pain patients—the pain patient will have withdrawal symptoms. [22]

Nevertheless, I have used it successfully for pain. If used for pain, you take it more frequently than for cravings. For pain, it only lasts about 6-8 hours. So it will need to be dosed every 6-8 hours. Some clinicians find benefit as high as 32 mg/day, with few seeing further benefit over this dose. However, some do well on 1-2 mg every 6-8 hours. So you see it is important to always start this medicine low and not to think a friend or relative's dose is right for you.

I also reduce pain with some other special interventions. Some of these include customized pain medications that go right through the skin near the pain's location. Some of these medical creams have up to six pain and inflammation medications rolled into one. Also, other mild to modest pain medications include misc. antidepressants and antiseizure medications, high dose omega 3 fatty acids, aggressive Vitamin D capsules or drops and sublingual compounded magnesium. Some of these latter options help 50% and some do nothing. You have to try them to know if they will help. If you are being treated for pure pain and not for opioid withdrawal, you do not count in the legal limit of 30 patients.

Because the DEA and Justice department fear narcotics being abused, *pain patients and their doctors are usually asked to document in **exhaustive and burdensome** detail,* the cause of their pain, and to accept some diagnostic studies and/or consults that support a pain cause. Unfortunately, this sadistic expectation of infinite pain medicine documentation, required by lawyers and overbearing government physicians, is effectively making a pain physician as common as a unicorn. This is done as many medical agencies report tens of millions in the United States have severe chronic pain.

Patients who need treatment for pain, but not for opioid dependence, can be treated with Suboxone for pain by any doctor. No certification is needed to use Suboxone or other forms of buprenorphine for pain. People with pain disorders should not be transferred to opioid treatment centers, just because they take opioids and have become physically dependent on the opioids for their **legitimate** pain.

Sometimes it is hard to distinguish between patients seeking pain relief and those who want to get "high." This is particularly true in patients who have both real pain and addiction issues. I am not convinced any agency or medical body has published a tool that truly separates these two groups. Though many ultra vigilant addictionologists and DEA officials are certain they can separate addiction and pain, particularly with "expert" unresearched checklists. **They forget the lessons of real war: under torture or ongoing pain, do not expect anyone to rise above "breaking."**

In the same way as the main figure in *Les Miserables* was willing to steal to stop the pain of hunger in his family, simplistic thinking would lead some to think that patients in horrible pain should simply be noble and stoic in the face of great pain. Some feel these criteria below are useful in separating pain patients from those who are addicted. I am not as sure.

Patients With Pain
Versus
Patients Who Are Addicted to Opioids [23]

Clinical Features	Patients With Pain	Patients Who Are Addicted to Opioids
Compulsive drug use	Rare	Common
Crave drug (when not in pain)	Rare	Common
Obtain or purchase drugs from non-medical sources	Rare	Common
Procure drugs through illegal activities	Absent	Common
Escalate opioid does without medical instruction	Rare	Common
Supplement with other opioid drugs	Unusual	Frequent
Demand specific opiod agent	Rare	Common
Can stop use when effective alternate treatments are available	Usually	Usually Not
Prefer specific routes of administration	No	Yes
Can regulate use according to supply	Yes	No

How Long Should I Stay on Suboxone?

Most patients do poorly rushing off Suboxone right after they are stabilized on a comfortable dose. I strongly urge you not to rush off Suboxone, even if you can do so safely. Why? If you have a real substance addiction problem, Suboxone will only remove your opioid cravings IF YOU TAKE IT.

Some studies have looked at relapse rates when people wean off Suboxone. **The highest relapsing rates are people who come off Suboxone immediately**. My impression is relapse rates decrease the longer you have been on maintenance. Perhaps this is because your brain has more time to recover from the effects of drug abuse, or you develop a wide range of satisfying activities and coping plans to handle drug temptations.

Should I Take Suboxone "As Needed" For Cravings?

Some patients have asked if they can just take Suboxone when the "urge" to use hits them. I oppose this thinking. First, it assumes that opioid dependence is really an easy think to handle, and it is as simple as using a hand cream for dry skin. Many patients have a period of excitement when they have a period of time with no cravings. This is a good thing to offer you hope. But it often does not last in the first two years, especially if you have contact with people, places and things from your past in which drugs are present.

This thinking also ignores the speed of drug lust. If you have an event that hurts you or depletes you emotionally or physically, you can be longing for an opioid release in **minutes.** But your Suboxone might not be on hand.

Also, Suboxone will not offer the tremendous high of an illegal or legal opioid. If you are really hurting, deeply bored or significantly depleted, you may wish for an explosive high, and not the calm contentment offered by Suboxone.

Finally, if you take Suboxone for a period of time and then plan to take "as needed," you will still need to decrease your dose slowly to allow a comfortable Suboxone detox.

Simply, I do not suggest this type of treatment.

Sample Reasons To Immediately Stop Suboxone

The following situations are serious and require promptly stopping your routine use of Suboxone: pregnancy, active alcohol dependence, impulsive or high-dose benzodiazepine dependence, jail, a new inability to afford the medication, the removal of a medical pain problem or opioid cravings even on 32 mg of Suboxone.

Pregnancy
If you are sexually active and not using two forms of birth control, do not be surprised if you become pregnant. Every form of birth control can fail at various rates, but if abstinence is not an option, a quality fresh synthetic condom, properly used, can help decrease pregnancy and the transmission of sexually transmitted diseases.

I have patients with children that were conceived with every form of birth control. Rare birth control failure rates are not "rare" if you are the one who gets pregnant. Further, birth control pills interact with hundreds of medications and the level of an effective synthetic birth control dose might fall too low. The frequency of these pregnancies is probably unknown. Discuss this with your OB or GYN physician. **Please notify your Suboxone prescriber and you OB/GYN physician and family doctor if you have a late period.**

The typical gold standard treatment, if you are pregnant, is to switch you from Suboxone to methadone. If you are on methadone at the time of your delivery, your child will need special treatment because they will be born with methadone in their system. Much has been written about how to address this withdrawal problem, and different physicians use different approaches.

One new technique, based on research at John's Hopkins, is to treat the mother with methadone, and then transition her to equal potency morphine which has a short duration in the body, and then transition her to pure buprenorphine (Subutex) or Suboxone. Initial impressions are that this is effective in preventing methadone infant withdrawals.

Alcohol Abuse
In France a number of individuals have died by combining IV buprenorphine and IV benzodiazapines. (Examples of benzodiazepines include Librium, Valium, Klonopin, Xanax and Ativan). In light of this experience, most physicians are concerned about any sedating drugs. Obviously, alcohol is a sedative and can cause respiratory depression. Buprenorphine can cause some respiratory depression or breathing slowness if used IV, and yet sublingually this appears to not be a problem. However, if you add very high doses of sedating agents or multiple sedating agents, there is a concern you might depress your respirations to the point of dying.

Most of us have seen individuals severely intoxicated. They have trouble walking. At times, they can have trouble breathing if they drink to an extreme. If they also have buprenorphine in their system, they are at much higher risk for fatal respiratory depression.

Some physicians will not place you on Suboxone if you have an alcohol dependence problem for this reason. They might realize you have this problem if you come to sessions with mints or a breath freshener on your breath, obvious intoxication, or various blood testing findings.

Some patients are just too hooked on alcohol to be on Suboxone. If you cannot abstain from alcohol, you need to have that problem addressed first. This might be with a specialist in addictions in an out patient setting, an in-patient rehabilitation center, at AA meetings or other treatment options. Once your drinking problem is addressed and stable, you can certainly reconsider taking Suboxone if you have opioid cravings.

High Dose Anti-anxiety Medications

Most training materials and agencies prefer you not use anxiety medications of the benzodiazapine class. As mentioned above, these would include Librium, Valium, Klonopin, Xanax and Ativan. The reason is a concern for respiratory depression that can be fatal. Physician's who are addictionologists tend to be the most avoidant of benzodiazepines.

Having said this, **many physicians will eventually prescribe these medications if other things fail,** even if some articles say it is contraindicated or not acceptable to do so with Suboxone. People with significant panic attacks, social anxiety and generalized anxiety are suffering from a real medical illness—one as real as major depression or diabetes, and should not have a treatment option withheld. This class of medications has been successfully used safely in millions of patients. We know from literature and history that millions of individuals have suffered with horrible panic, severe social anxiety and other anxiety problems. Panic attacks and social anxiety are not new. They should be treated seriously, and not trivialized and told it is a good thing "to feel." Of course we should all "feel," but panic attacks are not simple feeling, unless you consider being burned "feeling."

Some physicians and addiction counselors have seen individuals highly addicted to benzodiazapines. These individuals with benzodiazepine dependence take large amounts with no medical direction, in the same manner as some alcoholics who only stop drinking when they black out. These addiction counselors are correct in warning that this type of person is not able to handle benzodiazepines.

However, most people are able to handle anti-anxiety medications just fine, especially if the prescribing physician is careful and makes any dose increase slowly. And just because an anti-anxiety medication might need to be raised a couple times is not a reason to panic. Increasing a benzodiazepine under a doctor's care is first grade liver science and is NOT addiction.

Specifically, the liver increases its enzyme production to deal with any substance you eat regularly. The liver removes chemicals, herbs, toxins, medicines and food chemicals. So if you routinely take a herb or medication the number of enzymes used to remove it will increase, and you will need a higher dose of the herb or medication to have the **same blood level**. Further, the receptors that allow a medication like the benzodiazepines to work, can down regulate and become fewer in number, so to get the same calm effect, you often need to raise the dose 2-3x in the first year. This is also true of antidepressants, which few feel are "addictive" and yet their blood levels fall routinely each year and the receptors they hit can also decrease in number.

While I want to keep open the option of anxiety medications in some Suboxone patients, many physicians who prescribe anxiety medications usually want you to try some other options first, which do work in some people.

First, anti-depressants are mis-named because they have many effects. For example, they can reduce many forms of anxiety—10% to 100%. However, many physicians start antidepressants at doses that are far too high, and this alone can increase anxiety. Therefore, I generally suggest all antidepressants be started at 1/4-1/2 of the lowest dose during **day one**. You can increase the dose quickly according to your doctor's directions after day one. Having said this, some people do well with the published starting doses.

Antidepressants for anxiety should not be started at the full antidepressant doses, but instead they should be started at low doses used for anxiety—since they can be sedating. Some antidepressants with potent sedative/anti anxiety effects include:

* Trazodone

* Doxepin

* Elavil

Each of these is highly sedating at high anti-depressant doses, but at low doses sometimes they are useful for anxiety.

Also, some antidepressants are not good at helping pure anxiety. For example, Wellbutrin/Zyban which is buproprion is useful for depression but not for anxiety. SAMe or SAM-e is a natural antidepressant with many strong benefits but it is not helpful for anxiety (and you need to take a B-complex vitamin with it since these fall with use).

If you do not have panic attacks, and only have constant mild anxiety, either Gabatril or Buspar might offer some benefits. Both should be started at low doses, such as 2 mg at night for Gabatril and 5 mg per am for Buspar, but your doctor might have other suggestions.

Very low dose anti psychotic medications reduce panic attacks and anxiety. Some require an EKG during treatment to make sure the medication is safe for the heart. Some of these, such as Seroquel, can be started at very small doses such as 1/4 of a 25 mg tablets. (The dose for mania or schizophrenia is usually well over 400 mg).

Many types of counseling are directed at reducing excess anxiety. These do have some effectiveness. Even if they do not reduce your anxiety fully, they will usually help reduce it some amount.

Some physicians also want to make sure you have given yourself some time to get over the effects of your addiction(s), since almost all addictive substances increase depression and anxiety. The time between your last use of an abused substance until an anxiety medication trial is highly variable depending on the physician.

If you are prescribed anti-anxiety medications, please do not rush to high doses or "adjust" them yourself. You will typically be started at low doses to make sure you can tolerate them with Suboxone.

Below is a contract between you and your physician, if you are allowed to try anti-anxiety medications. It is also listed in the Appendix.

Benzodiazepine Treatment Contract [24]

I freely and voluntarily agree to accept this treatment contract, as follows:

1. I agree that the medication I receive is my responsibility and I will keep it in a safe, secure place. I understand that it is a felony to keep a benzodiazepine outside its properly labeled container as it is a controlled substance under the Controlled Substances Act 1970 21 U.S.C. §801 et seq. & sec 1308 Title 21 (CFR) Part 1300. I understand that these medications have a limited abuse liability, but that in my case, I may be at increased risk of abusing these medications.

2. If I loose my medication, I agree that the medication will not be replaced regardless of the reasons for such loss. It is my physician's responsibility to prohibit any abuse of these medications. I understand that these medications may cause very serious withdrawal symptoms including seizures, panic attacks, hallucinations and psychosis if stopped suddenly. If you experience one of these events, please proceed to your nearest emergency room.

3. I agree that my medication or prescriptions can only be given to me at my regular office visits. Any missed office visits will result in my not being able to get medication until the next scheduled visit.

    I agree not to obtain medications from any physicians, pharmacies, or other sources without informing my treating physician. Doing so may constitute fraud—a felony punishable by a prison sentence.

4. I understand that mixing benzodiazepines, such as Valium, Xanax, Ativan, Klonopin with alcohol or other drugs can be dangerous if not fatal. I understand that thousands of deaths have occurred among persons mixing benzodiazepine tranquilizers with alcohol, opioid narcotics and other drugs.

5. I agree to take my medication as the doctor has instructed, and not to alter the way I take my medication without first consulting the doctor. I agree not to exceed a daily dose of _____ unless expressly authorized by my doctor beforehand.

    My use of these medications will be supervised by ____
    _____.

6. I understand the medication alone may not be sufficient treatment for my disease, so I agree to participate in any patient education or Relapse Prevention program, as discussed, to assist me in my treatment and recovery.

7. I agree not to sell, share or give any of my medication to another person.

8. I agree to keep all my scheduled appointments with the
    doctor.

_____   _____
          Patient's signature   Date

_____   _____
          Witness signature   Date

Reasons to Stop Suboxone Continued

You are Going to Jail

Many jails are not just places of justice in which people lose their
freedom, but many have poor medical care. It seems to be another
type of punishment for the crimes the person has committed. I am
just speaking from my modest experience with jails in Collier County
Florida, and Delaware and Chester Counties in Pennsylvania. So stay
away from any illegal drug activities, since part of your punishment
will be sadistic and poor medical care in the prison.

Currently, jails do not offer Suboxone or any other medication treatment for opioid dependence. For example, even though our jails are
flooded with substance abusers, at present, Rikers Island in New York
City is the only correctional system in the United States that treats
heroin dependent inmates with methadone. [25]

Since Suboxone is more expensive than methadone, I doubt few will
argue for the expense of offering this to you in a jail. Therefore, if you
are going to jail, you should wean off it, just before you start serving
your time. Do not stop Suboxone months before you start serving
your time, because you will be too tempted to use illegal opioids. We
suggest an individualized detox plan designed specifically for you, using Suboxone in smaller and smaller doses, so that your final 2 mg
dose is the day before you report. Other physicians may have other
approaches.

Poverty

If you do not have prescription insurance, and can no longer afford Suboxone, you will need to taper off it.

Your Pain Source is Gone

If you have a pain source that is healed, such as a diseased knee joint that is replaced with an artificial joint, you might no longer need a pain medication or Suboxone for your pain. Therefore, you can wean off your Suboxone quite easily.

Seizure Medications Require Special Care

Barbiturates are sometimes used for problems like seizures. If they are going to be added to Suboxone or if you are already on them before starting Suboxone, your physicians will have to look at his interaction very closely. Some physicians will not want to have them combined—they worry about depressed breathing. Others will simply adjust your Suboxone or have your neurologist adjust your seizure medications. It is important that you and your physicians be aware that many seizure medications interact with buprenorphine and the level of either medication can go up or down.

A Possible Detoxification Plan

If you need to come off Suboxone for any of reasons mentioned above, you should not just suddenly stop it. Buprenorphine does cause a modest dependence and you can have some withdrawal symptoms if you suddenly stop it. Therefore, if you are going to stop Suboxone, one approach is to decrease your stable dose by 2 mg every couple days. Currently, there is no generally approved process for dose reduction. So discuss this with your physician.

Suboxone Cost

Most insurance plans cover Suboxone and so the cost to you would be any co-pay you would typically make for a medication that has no generic version. If you have to pay cash for your medications, here is the fee:

2 mg Size—Thirty Tablets is $89.81 average wholesale price

8 mg Size—Thirty Tablets is $158.94 average wholesale price

Typically a retail store will add 10-30% to this wholesale price. A 10% mark up is very small and would be typical of Costco, Sam's Club, Wal-Mart or BJ's. While they may have the best price, some of my patients have complained of poor customer service, long drop off or pick up lines, a limited ability to talk to the pharmacist, slow prescription preparation time and poor pharmacists. Perhaps the latter is due to low salaries for the pharmacists.

Smaller pharmacies might add 15-30% but they usually provide faster service, personal attention, assistance with other health issues, may ship your medications and have a willingness to call the physician to clarify possible interactions or anything that is unclear. They often can fill your prescription while you briefly shop. Further, some local pharmacies are also able to compound unique medications just for you. For example, we routinely prescribe special transdermal medications that go right through your skin to treat infections, diarrhea, nausea or vomiting, fever, joint pain, depression, cognitive slowing and nutrient depletions. If you asked for these special tailored items at a huge mega-store pharmacy or a large chain pharmacy, they would fall on the ground in laughter.

If you have to pay for Suboxone out of your own pocket, just recall, even if your Suboxone were to cost $20 per day, this is a fraction of the cost of a $200 per day oxycodone habit.

Not every pharmacy carries Suboxone. Some pharmacies refuse to carry Suboxone due to ignorance about its service to the community. Some pharmacists are highly opinionated and uninformed about modern clinical psychiatric and addiction care, and regard any controlled substance with contempt. They should be DEA agents and not pharmacists. Other pharmacists see the benefit of Suboxone, but do not want to deal with the burdensome paperwork.

I Still Have Opioid Craving with Suboxone

Most people dependent on opioids can probably be transitioned to Suboxone. However, some individuals require massive amounts of methadone to stop their cravings. These individuals will probably not be good candidates for Suboxone. Some manuals like patients at 30 mg of methadone for a week before starting Suboxone. All experts seem to agree you must be off methadone at least 1-2 days and have moderate withdrawal signs to make sure most of the methadone is gone. Individuals who need over 50 mg of methadone per day to prevent cravings for heroin, might not be ready for Suboxone. Suboxone probably cannot match this level of methadone, if it is really needed by the patient.

Methadone Release to Talk with Local Clinic

One critical issue when converting from methadone at any dose to Suboxone, is the methadone center and the Suboxone physician need formal releases to talk to each other—if they are not the same person. These "release of information" forms must meet both state and federal substance abuse treatment privacy laws.

Once a date for your final methadone dose is set, the clinic will need to confirm they are stopping methadone with the Suboxone physician.

Methadone at High Doses

While most patients on methadone can be converted to Suboxone, some might not be able to replace very high doses of methadone. Currently, most training plans like a patient on methadone to be on no more than 30 mg when they transition over to Suboxone. So what do you do if the person is on 75 mg of methadone?

First, it is not clear that everyone on high doses of methadone really need it. I have seen patients placed on 80 mg of methadone when the patient was relapsing with cocaine. Some centers feel high dose opioids helps you beat cocaine abuse, but this is not the required dose to prevent opioid abuse.

In some cases, I have seen patients slowly decreased to 30-40 mg and successfully transition to Suboxone. Of course if they have opioid cravings on 16-32 mg/day of Suboxone, they need to go back on methadone—the Suboxone is not strong enough or the methadone taper was too fast.

In one text, they discuss the successful use of Suboxone in a patient taking 80 mg of methadone. I have heard of rare patients taking 90 mg successfully transfer over, but this is a unique person and this high dose transition is not based on solid research. Generally, transitions from doses above 30-40 mg have higher failure rates.

If a person is likely to act out and use IV heroin or commit a crime to purchase pharmaceutical opioids, you should err on super close monitoring. One IV use could cause a HIV or hepatitis infection, and one purchase of some Percocet could result in an arrest.

If a patient is on high dose methadone, the first step is reducing the methadone **very slowly**. If you are on a high dose, rushing the methadone to 30 mg so you can be on Suboxone is an error. Rushing a methadone detox will merely make you feel uncomfortable physically, and will not give you time to get your social supports in place for a fully drug-free life. Do you want a successful experience? Then drop the methadone very slow. If you rush it, you may end up sabotaging your Suboxone trial.

Some studies feel that even slow methadone tapering can create a lust for opioids and lead to a relapse. We feel this is very valid. So if a person cannot handle a **very slow taper** to 30-40 mg of methadone, and has severe opioid cravings when on 75-100 mg of methadone, then they are probably not good candidates for Suboxone.

Some books suggest that the methadone be tapered to 30 mg, and then remain at this level for a full week, before a transition to Suboxone. I have not found that this is always required, and have successfully tapered patients who were at 30 mg of methadone for 36-48 hours, and while having mild-moderate withdrawal symptoms initiated Suboxone. With methadone, the recommended starting dose is small 2 mg units of Subutex, but many expert addictionologists use regular Suboxone. The buprenorphine 2 mg is repeated frequently, and then given in 4 mg units if the 2 mg are acceptable, up to a total of 16-32 mg a day. (A rare person sometimes does well on just 4 mg per day).

Some physicians get you to a high replacement dose in one day and others over three-four days. This high methadone replacement dose might be as high as 32 mg, but please realize this is not the standard recommended daily dose for Suboxone. It is just that some people benefit from a high dose at 32 mg. In any event, all major practitioners seem to agree no further benefit is derived from going higher than 32 mg/day for any use—opioid abuse prevention or pain control.

Dr. Michael Sheehan, a highly respected Tampa addiction expert, sometimes drops methadone in very small units if the patient is able to tolerate it. He reduces the dose until the person is unable to reduce it further, and then, if he sees clear withdrawal signs, **he adds some clonidine to take the edge off the withdrawal symptoms** to get a little more time and help the person with their discomfort. He and others use a wide range of symptomatic medications to help with nausea, diarrhea, muscle aches and other withdrawal problems. Since methadone stays in the body for days, partly because of a slow release from deep tissues, the longer the time before you start Suboxone, the better your chance of success. He is usually able to use clonidine and other medications to help the patient wait for 72 hours after their last methadone dose; then he adds a small amount of Suboxone. If the Suboxone does not suddenly worsen the situation, he gives them 16 mg day one, 24 mg day two and 32 mg day three.

As you see, different clinicians have different strategies.

So, in conclusion, some rare patients will still have opioid cravings with Suboxone as high as 32 mg per day. If these people were lowered very slowly on their methadone to 30 mg for a week, and still have opioid cravings on Suboxone 16-32 mg, it may mean they can only use methadone. Some patients require very high daily methadone to get a complete removal of their opioid cravings. While many patients on 50-60 mg of methadone can successfully use Suboxone, individuals who really need 90 mg, 100 mg or even 120 mg to block opioid cravings, should not ignore possible cravings that break through with Suboxone. If you have been tried on Suboxone after transitioning slowly down from high dose methadone, and you are lusting for street opioids, you are too high a risk for relapse. Any relapse is dangerous to your body and your liberty, so in your case methadone should be restored. [26-28]

Suboxone vs. Methadone on Decision Making

In one study, people were asked to perform different cognitive tests while on Suboxone or methadone. In general, Suboxone patients had better cognition and better decision-making. [29]

Cardiac Safety of Suboxone vs. Methadone

A rare but very dangerous arrhythmia was found in a patient taking methadone. The patient was transitioned to Suboxone and the cardiac problem stopped. [30]

Testosterone drops with Methadone vs. Suboxone

Testosterone has many important roles in the body. Some physicians feel these include building bone, preventing diabetes, opening blood vessels and helping people cope with stress. Methadone causes hypogonadism and reduced testosterone levels, particularly at higher doses. In contrast, Suboxone patients had testosterone blood levels equal to healthy people. Suboxone patients also complain of less sexual side effects. [31]

Suboxone and Other Addictions

Studies show that most folks using Suboxone for opioid addiction have other addictions. It matters which substances you are dependant on. It also matters if you are willing to address the addiction. For example, if you abuse high dose benzodiazepines, alcohol or barbiturates, most clinicians will think it is best for you to be stabilized before you go on Suboxone. For example, if your spouse fills for divorce, and you get very upset, and act out by drinking excessively or binging on benzodiazepines while also taking Suboxone, it is possible you could die. Both of these can depress breathing, and in acute or high doses can be dangerous with Suboxone.

However, if you abuse marijuana or stimulants, you probably **should** be on Suboxone, because of the risk to your body and liberty if you continue to abuse opioids, e.g. methadone, pharmaceutical pain medications or heroin. It is better for you to be on Suboxone than other more dangerous and illegal narcotics, which can cause up to a 10% death rate/year in some populations.

While I suggest a person abusing marijuana and stimulants be allowed access to Suboxone, please be aware that illegal substances of any kind can lead to arrests, and high potency stimulants are associated with liver damage, heart injury and strokes.

So during your intake, please let your Suboxone physician know which of these substances you struggle to control?

- Opiates
- Stimulants
- Sedative–Hypnotics
- Anabolic Steroids
- Marijuana
- Phencyclidine (PCP)
- Hallucinogens
- Alcohol
- Nicotine
- Inhalants

Will I Be Addicted to Suboxone?

Taking Suboxone under the tongue will create a mild-modest dependence on Suboxone. Individuals who develop a significant dependence on the active ingredient, buprenorphine, seem to get this dependence from grinding it up and using it IV. Dependence on Suboxone, when taken correctly under the tongue, does not result in severe opioid withdrawals, but you can have mild to modest withdrawal.

Suboxone Side Effects

The active ingredient of Suboxone has been used for over twenty years around the world. The following are some possible side effects from my research and experience with this medication. Some studies do not show more than a few side effects, and other lists show a larger number. I have not routinely had patients experience many side effects when the treatment is started slow and carefully, and with very good communication with the doctor throughout day one and two.

* Constipation

* Nausea

* Vomiting

* Headache

* Pain

* Insomnia

* Sweating

* Drowsiness—so be extra careful with your dosing, especially during your first few days. You must be alert if you are driving, using heavy machinery, going on ladders or up on high places.

* Itch

* Dry mouth

* Pupil contraction (narrow pupils)

* Dizziness with sudden standing

* Male ejaculation trouble

* Urine retention

* Withdrawal feelings

* Rare liver damage is possible and described below

* Rare jaundice or yellowing of skin or eyes (requires immediate emergency care)

* Shortness of breath needs to be evaluated promptly, especially if you have been drinking alcohol, taken sedating medications such as some antidepressants, benzodiazepine anti-anxiety medications, seizure medications, tranquilizers or an increased or high dose of Suboxone.

* Allergic reactions are possible and include difficulty breathing, hives, swelling, asthma, wheezing, dangerously low blood pressure or loss of consciousness. [32]

Rare Eccentric Reactions

Since I do a little pain medicine, I have used Suboxone in a few people with pain. Some have done amazing. One doctor who failed 35-40 medications from 15 different physicians lost a terrible migraine with 2 mg of Suboxone a day. Yet when I have tried to treat others for pain, I think one subgroup does poorly. I have found that individuals with neurological Lyme disease, Bartonella (cat scratch fever from tiny ticks or cats), Ehrlichia or significant indoor mold exposure might be more sensitive to the medication and react badly to it—their pain got worse, they got agitated and they were miserable. This has happened with three patients on 2-4 mg of Suboxone who were not on previous opioids.

Risks of Suboxone Use [33]

One brief table below lists some sample risks.

Some Sample Conditions in Which Buprenorphine Must Be Used With Caution	
Condition	**Reason for Caution**
Severe liver impairment	Decreased metabolism of the medication, higher plasma concentrations
Severe kidney impairment	Decreased elimination of the medication, higher plasma concentrations
Severe lung impairment	Increased respiratory depression risk in which breathing is too low to live
Severe scoliosis or a humpback spine	Increased respiratory depression risk in which breathing is too low to live
Low thyroid hormone Low cortisol hormone Brain impairment or coma Psychosis Intoxication with alcohol Intoxication with benzodiazapines Delirium tremens from alcohol withdrawal	Decreases brain functioning
Head injury	May increase cerebrospinal pressure; may obscure diagnosis by decreased pain
Prostatic hypertrophy or enlargement or urethral stricture	Decreased ability to urinate
Pregnancy	Category C, need a risk/benefit assessment; may cause neonatal withdrawal
Dysfunction of the biliary tract	Risk of increased biliary tract pressure which could be a medical emergency
Infectious or inflamed belly conditions	May obscure diagnosis or clinical course by removing pain

Depressed Respirations

* Significant respiratory depression that can cause death has occurred with the combination of IV buprenorphine and sedatives such as alcohol, other opioids or barbiturates.

* Mixing Suboxone with oral benzodiazapines or alcohol offers a potential danger. Do not take any dose of benzodiazepines without understanding that this poses some unknown health risk.

* Do not drink alcohol while on Suboxone.

* Some individuals already have respiratory problems and adding Suboxone may make a respiratory problem worse. Therefore, Suboxone must be used with caution in patients who have a risk of respiratory disease. These patients who are at some risk with Suboxone are smokers, individuals with COPD or chronic obstructive pulmonary disease, cor pulmonale, abnormal pulmonary function tests, decreased pulmonary reserve, respiratory depression from other causes, hypoxia, hypercapnia, apnea, some sleep disorders and lung cancer.

Brain Functioning Depression
If you add Suboxone to medications that depress the brain's functioning, it is possible you can have lowered alertness. This can put you at risk on stairs, during any driving or if you are working on high places, e.g., on a ladder or roof. The following types of medications are samples of those that lower brain activity or alertness: narcotics or strong painkillers, anesthetics which put you to sleep during operations, anti-anxiety medications (benzodiazepines), anti-psychotic medications like phenothiazines, barbiturates, mania medications, sleep medications and alcohol.

You and your physician should be aware of this possible increased problem of two sedating substances and adjust your medications if possible.

Opioid Dependence

Buprenorphine is a pain medication that **partially** stimulates the same pain receptors as other painkillers. If Suboxone is used chronically, dependence is common and withdrawal signs and symptoms are possible, especially if you suddenly stop or decrease your medication. However, since this is a partial pain receptor medication, the withdrawal is less than full agonists like methadone or oxycodone.

Liver Risks

Individuals with a history of addiction have been found to have various types of hepatitis. Sometimes this includes yellowing of the skin or jaundice, increased liver lab abnormalities, liver failure and liver death. Many physicians feel most of these liver problems were associated with pre-existing liver trouble before the use of Suboxone. For example, individuals with hepatitis B or C, or IV drug use have clear reasons for an injured liver with Suboxone use. However, in other rare patients it is not easy find a reason for the liver damage. Therefore, consider that Suboxone has some small risk of liver injury and get liver function test labs done if your physician orders them—before treatment and after you start treatment. No set frequency is established.

If you ever turn yellow go to an emergency department.

Other Risks

Individuals can have allergic reactions to either buprenorphine or naloxone. Typical problems include itching, various rashes, hives, throat narrowing, dangerous swelling and shock. If you are allergic to either buprenorphine or naloxone, do not restart it without the support of an expert allergist.

Injury Risk

Because Suboxone has some sedating side effects, you have to extra careful that you are alert enough to operate machinery, such as a lawn mower, car, motorcycle or industrial equipment. If you increase your dose or add a drug which can interact with Suboxone or which has sedating properties, be extra careful to look for new sedation and new impairment.

Blood Pressure

All opioids can lower blood pressure. Since buprenorphine has partial opioid features, it can lower blood pressure. Therefore all patients on buprenorphene should be alert to dizziness and blood pressure changes when standing from a laying or sitting position. Report this to your doctor immediately.

Intracranial Pressure

All opioids can possibly increase the pressure inside the head. Therefore, buprenorphine should be used very carefully if someone has brain injury in their past. Specifically, individuals with seizures, past periods of lost consciousness, head injuries, positive signs of brain tissue damage, e.g., such as might be found on a CT Scan, MRI or neurology exam, should use Suboxone with extra caution. Any history of increased intracranial pressure requires extra vigilance with buprenorphine.

Buprenorphine can alter vision, so this should be kept in mind when optimal vision is required. If your vision is altered in a manner that is unsafe, call both your treating physician and get a consult with an eye physician.

Patients with Significant Medical Illness

Patients who are frail, elderly or have significant medical illnesses require extra caution before being treated with buprenorphine. For example, liver disease may alter blood levels of either buprenorphine or naloxone. Individuals with diseases of the biliary tract need close monitoring since buprenorphene can alter the pressure in the bile system.

Since Suboxone reduces pain, it is possible it might decrease your awareness of a broken bone, a mild heart attack or abdominal disease.

Informing Emergency Room Personnel and Significant Others

In the event you are in an accident and lose consciousness, it might be good to have on your person two cards informing the ER staff you are on Suboxone and any other critical medical illnesses you have and your medications.

For example, one sample card might say this for Mr. Jones:

Dear Emergency Room Staff

I take 8 mg of Suboxone each 8 AM and 2 PM

My other medications are:

> **1) Effexor XR 150 mg capsules am and bed**
> **2) Metformin 1000 mg am and night**
> **3) B Complex Vitamin**

I have adult onset diabetes, and hypertension and a metal rod in my femur from a severe fall 3/06.

I am allergic to amoxicillin – my throat closes up if I take it.

(Sign your name, print your name and date on the card).

*****

We would also suggest you tell your most trusted family and friends that you take Suboxone in case you become unconscious and can not tell anyone. Why? Suboxone alters many medication blood levels, and it would help the emergency room physicians to know this information.

Medical Emergency Pain Care

If you are injured or develop a severe pain problem, e.g., a broken leg, kidney stone or appendicitis, then the pain will probably become higher than the anti-pain effects of Suboxone. If you break a bone or have a new and severe pain problem, do not take any Suboxone, because the emergency room staff will need to treat you with short acting opioids. Often, the doses needed in the presence of residual Suboxone and with a past history of opioid abuse, are very high. However, as the buprenorphine leaves the body, you will usually require less pain medication since the opioid will be more effective. [34]

Overdose Reactions

If you mix multiple sedating agents, your respirations could become dangerously low. This is especially true if you combine a high dose of Suboxone with high amounts of benzodiazepines, sedatives, barbiturates, seizure medications, antidepressants, or alcohol containing beverages.

Keep A Medication List

Since buprenorphine interacts with some medications, you should keep an accurate list of any other medications you are taking. This list should have the name, the pill size and how you take it. Give a copy to any physician who is treating you.

Cancer and Fertility Issues

Currently, it does not appear that buprenorphine causes cancer. Other studies will follow up and address this issue.

Pregnancy Issues

The current practice of most physicians is to switch from Suboxone to methadone if you are pregnant. Suboxone is a category C medication. The basic meaning of a C medication is that animal studies have shown adverse effects on the fetus or embryo, and there are no controlled studies on women. Some high dose animal studies seem to show possible trouble with having a fertilized egg implant and grow successfully in the uterine wall. Some physicians would use buprenorphine if the benefits clearly outweighed the risks.

Infant Withdrawal

If a women is taking buprenorphine when she delivers her child, it is possible the child will have some opioid withdrawal signs on day 1-8. Usually, these appear soon after delivery, and common infant signs include excessive reflexes, restlessness, tremor, jerking and rare seizures.

Breast Milk

Buprenorphine passes into the mother's milk. We do not have any real data to tell us how this will impact small infants. Therefore, breast-feeding is not recommended in women taking Suboxone.

Suboxone Use in Children

Some physicians have used buprenorphine with children. Little research has been done to prove it is safe to use in children. However, one new study of 36 opiate-dependent adolescents (aged 13-18) showed over 28 days that Suboxone was significantly superior to Catapress (clonidine) in these children. In conclusion, if Suboxone is going to be used in a child or young adolescent, a parent and/or patient should look at the risks and benefits. One risk being that few studies exist in children. [35, 36]

Suboxone and Drug Interactions

Suboxone is partly removed from the body by a special part of the liver called the CYP 3A4 system. While this is an unusual complex name, all it means is that a certain set of enzymes are able to "catch" this drug and remove it, in the same way a baseball is caught by a glove in baseball. So why even mention this enzyme?

Simply, so you and your doctor can be alert to drug interactions. Other medications such as anti-fungals, antibiotics, antiseizure agents and especially HIV medications interact with Suboxone. Some of these interactions cause either Suboxone to increase or decrease, or the other medication to do the same. Frankly, for most medications that use this enzyme system, we have little data to know how Suboxone will interact. So if you take medications on this list below, you and your doctor should be careful. Also, this list will need to be updated yearly.

A Sample List of Medications
Metabolized by CytoP450 3A4 [37]

Inhibitors (potentially increasing blood levels of buprenorphine)	Substrates		Inducers (potentially decreasing blood levels of buprenorphine)
Amiodarone	Alprazolam	Loratadine	Carbamazepine
Clarithromycin	Amlodipine	Losartan	Dexamethasone
Delavirdine	Astemizole	Lovastatin	Efavirenz
Erythromycin	Atorvastatin	Miconazole	Ethosuximide
Fluconazole	Carbamazepine	Midazolam	Nevirapine
Fluoxetine	Cisapride	Navelbine	Phenobarbital
Fluvoxamine	Clindamycin	Nefazadone	Phenytoin
Grapefruit Juice	Clonazepam	Nelfinavir	Primadone
Indinavir	Cyclobenzaprine	Nicardipine	Rifampin
Itraconazole	Cyclosporine	Nifedipine	
Ketoconazole	Dapsone	Nimodipine	
Metronidazole	Delavirdine	Ondansetron	
Miconazole	Dexamethasone	Oral Contraceptives	
Nefazadone	Diazepam	Paclitaxel	
Nelfinavir	Diltiazem	Prednisone	
Nicardipine	Disopyramide	Progestins	
Norfloxacin	Doxorubicin	Quinidine	
Omeprozol	Erythromycin	Rifampin	
Paroxetine	Estrogens	Ritonavir	
Ritonavir	Etoposide	(R) Warfarin	
Saquinavir	Felodipine	Saquinavir	
Sertraline	Fentanyl	Sertraline	
Verapamil	Fexofenadine	Simvastatin	
Zafirlukast	Glyburide	Tacrolimus	
Zileuton	Ifosfamide	Tamoxifen	
	Indinavir	Verapamil	
	Ketoconazole	Vinblastine	
	Lansoprazole	Zileuton	
	Lidocaine		

For a continuously updated list of cytochrome P450 3A4 drug interactions, visit http://medicine.iupui.edu/flockhart/table.htm.

Your Physician's Requirements For Treatment

Sometimes you might be confused by all the questions your doctor is asking. You might feel frustrated and just wish you could simply get your prescription. After your intake the questions and hassle should drop markedly.

Yet your doctor has some goals to achieve to offer you the best care:

1) Your doctor has to learn your past and present substance abuse history, surgical history and medical history.

2) They need to order a lab evaluation.

3) They need to do some type of physical exam—each type of doctor does a different style exam.

4) Some might use paper and pencil scales to measure your level of dependence.

5) Previous treatments for your opioid addiction and the outcome.

6) They need to explore any psychiatric history and treatments.

7) They should determine your genetic family risk for substance abuse and other medical problems.

8) Your current legal and illegal current medications.

9) A sexual history and a pregnancy history

10) Can you work, go to school or care for your children?

11) Does your support network bring you down emotionally and make you want to abuse drugs, or do they help your recovery?

12) Are you ready to change and try to live in a healthy drug-free manner?

13) Do you really want Suboxone? Do you understand the risks and benefits? Do you understand the risks if you take your past opioids while on Suboxone? The physician has to be sure you really want it and they are not forcing you to take it.

While I oppose the ridiculous documentation expectations of malpractice lawyers, state board members, pseudo-experts and physician "guideline" makers in terms of their entitlement and expectation for infinite documentation—paperwork which requires so much detail all rapport with you will be lost. I do, nevertheless, think clinicians should generally try to be aware of these thirteen issues above in a person using Suboxone. However, I am not saying these thirteen things should be made a requirement.

Looking At Your Body: Is It Telling You to Change? [38]

Using legal and illegal drugs in a dependent manner can lead to a poor appearance, a less appealing personality and deteriorating health. Below is a sample of body problems or signs associated with substance use. Do you want these things to be part of who you are in three years?

- **Your Overall Body:**
  Odor of alcohol on breath
  Odor of marijuana on clothing
  Odor of nicotine or smoke on breath or clothing
  Poor nutritional status
  Poor personal hygiene

- **Your Behavior in the Last Three Months:**
  Intoxicated behavior
  Slurred speech
  Staggering gait

- **Skin:**
  Signs of physical injury
  Bruises
  Lacerations
  Scratches
  Burns
  Needle marks
  Skin abscesses
  Skin infections
  Jaundice
  Palm redness
  Hair loss
  Sweating
  Rash
  Puffy hands

- **Head, Eyes, Ears, Nose, Throat:**
  Red eyes
  Inflamed nasal passages
  Perforated nasal septum
  Worn nasal septum
  Sinus tenderness
  Gum disease, gingivitis
  Gingival ulceration
  A runny nose
  Infected sinuses
  Pale mucus membranes
  Burns in oral cavity

- **Intestinal Tract:**
  Enlarged liver
  Liver tenderness
  Microscopic blood in your stool

- **Immune Problems:**
  Swollen or big lymph nodes

- **Heart and Blood Vessels:**
  High blood pressure
  Rapid heart rate
  Heart arrhythmia
  Heart valve disease
  Swelling

- **Lungs**
  Wheezing and other breathing sounds
  Cough
  Shortness of breath

- **Female reproductive:**
  Pelvic tenderness
  Vaginal discharge

- **Male reproductive:**
  Testis shrink
  Penile discharge
  Male fatty breasts

- **Neuron Health:**
  Senses impaired
  Memory impaired
  Muscle problems
  Eye movement trouble
  Nerve injury
  Tremor
  Thinking deficits
  Altered walking
  Eye's dilated or constricted

Recommended Baseline Laboratory Evaluation [38]

Laboratory testing is an important part of the assessment and evaluation of patients who have an addiction. Laboratory tests cannot make a diagnosis of addiction, but a variety of laboratory evaluations are useful in the assessment of patients who have an addiction. The recommended baseline laboratory evaluation of patients who are addicted to opioids is shown below.

- Serum electrolytes
- BUN and creatinine
- CBC with differential and platelet count
- Liver function tests (GGT, AST, ALT, PT, albumin)
- Lipid profile
- Urinalysis

- Pregnancy test (for women of childbearing age)
- Toxicology tests for drugs of abuse
- Hepatitis B and C screens

The following additional laboratory evaluations should be considered and offered as indicated:

- Blood alcohol level (using a breath testing instrument or a blood sample)

- Infectious disease evaluation:
  - HIV antibody testing
  - Hepatitis B virus (HBV) and hepatitis C virus (HCV) screens
  - Serology test for syphilis Venereal Disease Research Laboratories (VDRL)
  - Purified protein derivative (PPD) test for tuberculosis, preferably with control skin tests

Other Possible Lab Tests

I have found that individuals with Lyme, Babesia or Bartonella are highly prone to act out with substances. These are very common illnesses carried by poppy-seed size ticks, larger ticks or other insects and animals. Some debate exists in the medical community over the best labs to use for testing these infections. I offer extensive free information on this debate on www.personalconsult.com. We have found many individuals who had one or more of these infections who were negative by CDC criteria and common lab companies, who became positive on the third or even the sixth test.

I have also found that opioid addicted individuals can have abnormal hormones that influence contentment, energy, body aches, satisfaction and joy. These sample labs include MSH, VIP, VEGF, erythro-

poietin and a dozen others. These are discussed in deta
books, e.g., *Mold Illness Made Simple: Fixing Sick Bod
ings*. (It is available on Amazon.com, your local bookstore or on <u>www. usmoldphysician.com</u> as a $4.95 download).

How Do I Find a Suboxone Certified Physician?

You can log onto this link and find the name, address and phone number of those who are certified: http://buprenorphine.samhsa. gov/bwns_locator/index.html or insert the words in your search toolbar, "SAMHSA Buprenorphine Physician Locator" and you will be referred to a list. One limitation of the list is it only allows one zip code for each physician. Therefore, you might have a few more physicians in your area then are listed. Also, some doctors choose not to be listed, perhaps because their work gives them thirty patients, or they do not want a large Suboxone practice due to fear of the government for using a partial opioid agonist or partial pain medication. (The government has declared "war" on pain physicians using opioids for chronic pain).

If you do not have a computer, you can probably get help from the main Suboxone web site phone numbers: 877.782.6966 or 877 SUB-OXONE.

SCHALLEY

A Physician's Suboxone Treatment Checklist [40]

(Write Y or N)

This helps confirm you are a good candidate for Suboxone and it lists some basic things a patient should know.

1. Does the patient have a diagnosis of opioid dependence? _____

2. Are there current signs of intoxication or withdrawal? Is there a risk for severe withdrawal? _____

3. Is the patient interested in buprenorphine treatment? _____

4. Does the patient understand the risks and benefits of buprenorphine treatment? _____

5. Can the patient be expected to adhere to the treatment plan? _____

6. Is the patient willing and able to follow safety procedures? _____

7. Does the patient agree to treatment after a review of the options? _____

8. Can other drug recovery treatments besides Suboxone, be provided by the physician or by others? _____

9. Is the patient psychiatrically stable? Is the patient actively suicidal or homicidal; has he or she recently attempted suicide or homicide? Does the patient exhibit emotional, behavioral, or cognitive conditions that complicate treatment? _____

10. Is the patient pregnant? _____

11. Is the patient currently dependent on or abusing alcohol? _____

12. Is the patient currently dependent on benzodiazepines, barbiturates, or other sedative-hypnotics? _____

13. What is the patient's risk for continued opioid use or continued problems? Does the patient have a history of multiple previous treatments or relapses, or is the patient at high risk for relapse to opioid use? Is the patient using other drugs? _____

14. Has the patient had prior adverse reactions to buprenorphine? _____

15 Is the patient taking other medications that may interact with buprenorphine? _____

16. Does the patient have medical problems that prevent buprenorphine treatment? Are there physical illnesses that complicate treatment? _____

17. What kind of recovery environment does the patient have? Are the patient's psychosocial circumstances sufficiently stable and supportive? _____

18. What is the patient's level of motivation? _____
    (Y = sufficient or %)

Patient Name _____   Date _____

Physician Signature _____

Physician Insurance Coding Help

Here are some sample diagnostic codes that might be of use in insurance billing so that you might get some refund for your medical care. Unfortunately, many Suboxone physicians do not take insurance, and if they provide a receipt, the "customary and reasonable" rates your insurance company will approve are from 1920.

ICD-9 Opioid Related Codes

- Opioid Abuse (305.50)
- Opioid Dependence (304.00)
- Opioid Withdrawal (292.0)
- Opioid-Related Disorder NOS (292.9)

Source: International Classification of Diseases, 9th Rev., Clinical Modification: ICD -9 -CM. Volumes 1 and 2. Salt Lake City, UT: Ingenix, Medicode, 2003.

ICD -9 Other Sample Substance Abuse Codes

- 305.01 Alcohol abuse, continuous
- 305.02 Alcohol abuse, episodic
- 305.03 Alcohol abuse, remission
- 305.00 Alcohol abuse, unspec.
- 303.91 Alcoholism, chronic, continuous
- 304.41 Amphetamine dependence, continuous
- 304.11 Barbiturate dependence, continuous
- 305.22 Cannabis abuse, episodic
- 304.31 Cannabis dependence, continuous
- 305.62 Cocaine abuse, episodic
- 304.21 Cocaine dependence, continuous

Source for this brief quote: Diagnostic and Statistical Manual of Mental Disorders, 4th ed., Text Revision. Copyright 2000. (American Psychiatric Association 2000).

Consent to Release of Information

The privacy and confidentiality of individually identifiable drug or alcohol treatment information is protected by SAMHSA confidentiality regulation Title 42, Part 2 of the Code of Federal Regulations (42 C.F.R. Part 2). This regulation requires that physicians providing opioid addiction treatment obtain signed patient consent before disclosing individually identifiable addiction treatment information to any third party. Below is a sample consent form for a pharmacy containing all the data elements required by 42 C.F.R. Part 2.

Release of Information to a Pharmacy Filling a Suboxone Prescription

1. I (name of patient) _____

2. Authorize: Dr. _____

3. To disclose: (kind and amount of information to be disclosed)

    Any information needed to confirm the validity of my prescription and for submission for payment for the prescription.

4. To: (name or title of the individual or organization to which disclosure is to be made)

    The dispensing pharmacy to which I present my prescription or to which my prescription is called/ sent/faxed, as well as to third party payers.

5. For (purpose of the disclosure)

   **Assuring the pharmacy of the validity of the pre-
   scription, so it can be legally dispensed, and for
   payment purposes.**

6. Date (on which this consent is signed) _____

7. Signature of patient _____

8. Signature of parent or guardian (where required)

   _____

9. Signature of individual authorized to sign in lieu of the
   patient (where required) _____

This consent is subject to revocation at any time except to the extent
that the program which is to make the disclosure has already taken
action in reliance on it. If not previously revoked, this consent will terminate on: (specific date, event, or condition). _____

_____

This information has been disclosed to you from records protected by
Federal confidentiality rules (Title 42, Part 2, Code of Federal Regulations [42 C.F.R. Part 2]). The Federal rules prohibit you from making
any further disclosure of this information unless further disclosure is
expressly permitted by the written consent of the individual to whom
it pertains or as otherwise permitted by 42 C.F.R. Part 2. A general
authorization for the release of medical or other information is NOT
sufficient for this purpose.

Emergency Opioid Intoxication and Overdose

It is well known that opioids have the capacity to cause fatalities especially if new impulsive high doses are taken and added to impulsively increased sedatives or alcohol. Thankfully, individuals using opioids for both acute and chronic pain do very well. But individuals using heroin and other opioids abusively are at risk. Why? The drug they use can vary in potency, the amount taken can be suddenly increased or they can impulsively add other sedating medications like alcohol or barbiturates. Therefore, both patients and physicians should be aware of the danger signs.

On the table below I offer tools to determine if a person is in the midst of an opioid intoxication or overdose.

Signs of Opioid Intoxication and Overdose [41]

Syndrome	Physical Findings
Opioid Intoxication	Conscious Sedated Drowsy Slurred speech "Nodding" or intermittently dozing Memory impairment Mood — normal to euphoric Pupillary constriction
Opioid Overdose	Unconscious Pinpoint pupils Slow and shallow respirations Respirations below 10 per minute Pulse rate below 40 per minute

Anyone with signs of opioid overdose must be transported to an emergency room immediately. Call 911 or your local emergency medical number. *Do not delay.*

Emergency Treatment: Emergency Room Physicians

If someone takes an overdose of Suboxone, the first treatment goal is making sure they have clearly established ventilation. This may require a mechanical respirator to achieve successful respirations. Medications like naloxone, which are anti-opioids, may not be effective in reversing respiratory depressions produced by an overdose of buprenorphine.

If an emergency room physician is recommending mechanical ventilation, they are simply trying to be helpful.

Non-Medical Opioid Treatment

Counseling and Group Therapy Options

The treatment of an addiction involves more than a pill. Some medications are very useful in helping a person to remain free from addiction, but I would suggest that other treatments be added to your Suboxone care. Your Suboxone physician might offer some of these treatments or refer you to others to do them. Please accept any referrals you are given. Here are some sample treatments to insure success with Suboxone.

1) **Simple Supportive "Talk" Therapy**—If all your friends were individuals who abused drugs, you will need to cut your connection to them to be successful in your recovery. So you might be lonely for a time before you find new relationships. A therapist can help provide a safe place to express your feelings, and to help you avoid dangerous decisions or actions.

2) **Cognitive Behavior Therapy**—When you are medically ill or ill from an addiction it is easy to start thinking primitively. This type of immature thinking involves seeing people as either friends or enemies, saints or devils or some other type of extreme. Events are either catastrophes or fantastic days. One loses the ability to think in grays. The therapist has you look at your current situations to see them realistically without excess extremes.

3) **Group Therapy**—Dozens of types of groups exist and so it is likely that with some work and exploration you might be able to find one that fits you. Your group may be folks trying to avoid substances like NA, AA or a small group meeting with an addiction counselor. It might also be people who are involved in one of your interests, e.g, photography, dogs, remote control airplanes, Habitat for Hu-

manity, mechanical hobbies or a church group. As long as it makes your recovery stronger, it can be a useful group.

4) **Detoxification of Other Drugs**—sometimes people are not aware or honest with their drug use. But after being on Suboxone and seeing it work they get hopeful that they might actually be able to come off another addictive substance. Other's find they are too sedated with their other addictive substance, e.g., alcohol added to Suboxone. So they need to do a detox from their high alcohol use first, in order to allow the Suboxone to work. Detoxification can be done in days in an in-patient facility or as an outpatient. I think it is better to have closer monitoring and to do in-patient detox, but that is between you and your physician or addiction specialist.

5) **Relapse Training**—the addiction field has been exposed to millions of people addicted to virtually everything possible. They have found clear triggers for relapse and clear things that help you stay clean and healthy. These principles can be learned in groups or simply taught like one would learn basic addition. While these are easy to learn, many make the mistake of thinking they are obvious. They are not obvious insights.

6) **Motivational Enhancement Therapy (MET)**—In this type of treatment a therapist sizes up your risk of relapse and offers feedback to fuel your motivation to help with your change process. MET believes you are capable of changing your behavior. The MET therapist believes you have inner resources that can be used to prevent relapse. In MET, the therapist is strongly empathetic, avoids debating, and examines the pros and cons of your drug use. They focus on where you are and where you want to be in the future.

7) **Family Therapy**—If you are a parent and have abused substances it is very likely you have made some mistakes. If you have had trouble with your parents or siblings, family therapy might be a place to remove relational triggers to abuse drugs. Some people should not consider family therapy early in their recovery, because it would upset them too much. They might do better with it at a much later time. Discuss this with a professional counselor.

8) **Psychiatric Medical Treatment**—research shows that many individuals with opioid cravings also have other psychiatric struggles like depression, panic attacks, general anxiety and other problems. Try to avoid false guilt if you end up needing medication to help depression or anxiety disorders. These psychiatric disorders can be as biological as diabetes.

9) **Vocational Counseling**—If you have a job or activity that is meaningful and which pays the bills it will help you to stay away from destructive substances. Vocational therapy experts can look at your interests, skills, passions and education, and help you think of a plan to make a good living. However, please understand that it might be months or a couple seasons before you naturally develop interests besides substance abuse.

Relapse Reflection Questions

Some people benefit from looking at triggers that might cause them
to relapse. Look over these questions to see what I mean.

1) Are you using substances to handle or numb unpleasant
   feelings or fatigue?

2) Are you using substances to remove emotional or physical
   pain?

3) Do you use substances to allow you to relate better? Do
   you feel less shy when you take substances?

4) Are you relaxed on substances?

5) Do you feel energetic and smart and capable when you use
   substances?

6) What feelings do substances ward off?

7) What is your goal in using substances?

8) What is your worst memory of substance use?

9) What have been one or two good experiences with substances?

10) How has your life been put on hold by substance abuse?

11) What are the risks or benefits of using any substance you
    "love" or "like" again for a month or a year?

12) How long do you think you can use this substance before
    trouble starts for you?

13) Why did you stop?

14) Do you think it is easy to stop using if you relapse?

Comprehensive Medical Opioid Addiction Assessment
Part of a Complete Recovery

While it is impossible to routinely ask each of these questions below, it is useful to be aware of the general categories. A physician prescribing Suboxone might try to become aware of these important patient concerns. In the same way, if you who want to take Suboxone or are already taking it, you might benefit from looking at some of these important questions. If you feel some topic was neglected in your intake, please let the physician know.

History of Drug Use

What substances have been used over time? Begin with the first psychoactive substance used (licit or illicit, prescribed or nonprescribed), including nicotine and caffeine. Ask about the first use of all drugs: age at first use, drugs used, description of the experiences and the situations, amounts used, feelings, complications, and results. "How old were you when you first tried alcohol or any other drugs? Describe the experience to me."

Ask about all psychoactive substances:

Alcohol	Nicotine
Amphetamines	Opioids
Caffeine	Phencyclidine (PCP)
Cannabis	Sedatives
Cocaine	Hypnotics or sleep medications
Hallucinogens	Anti-anxiety medications
Inhalants	Others

What substances has the patient ever used? When were each of these first used? What were the effects? What has happened over time? Focus on opioid use, progression of problems, and recent symptoms in patients being considered for buprenorphine treatment.

Effects of the Drugs Over Time

Explore the pattern of use of each substance. What has been the evolution and progression of use over time? Determine the frequency of use, amount of drugs used, route(s) used, progression of symptoms, and social context(s) of use. Has the patient attempted to cut down or control use; taken greater amounts of drugs or over a longer period than intended; spent much time using, obtaining drugs, or recovering from use? Has the patient had blackouts, shakes, withdrawal symptoms, compulsivity of use, and/or craving? Has he or she injected drugs; reduced or abandoned important activities as a consequence of use; and/or continued to use despite problems or consequences? If so, give examples.

When did regular opioid use begin? Does the patient have to use to feel "normal"? Describe periods of heaviest use. Explore in detail the pattern of use during the weeks prior to evaluation, including the amount and time of last use. When did he or she last consume alcohol or ingest or inject drugs? What was used? How much? What were the effects of the last drugs used?

Tolerance, Intoxication, and Withdrawal

For each drug ever used, explore tolerance, intoxication, and withdrawal syndromes. Especially focus on opioid-related syndromes.

Tolerance is the need for markedly increased amounts of the substance to achieve intoxication or desired effect, or markedly diminished effect with continued use of the same amount of the substance.

- Has tolerance developed to any drugs of abuse? How has tolerance manifested in this patient? Has any decrease in tolerance occurred? Quantify tolerance by the amount used and/or the cost of drugs needed to achieve effects.

- What is the most of each substance the patient can consume in a 24 -hour period now?

Intoxication and Overdose
- Explore symptoms of intoxication for each drug used.

- **Intoxication**. What was the patient's age at first intoxication? What drug(s) were involved in that intoxication? How have intoxication episodes progressed over time? Describe recent intoxication episodes.
- For opioids, has the patient experienced drowsiness ("nodding out"), slurred speech, impaired memory or attention, respiratory depression, and/or coma?

- **Overdose**. Have there been any episodes of intentional or nonintentional overdose with any drug or drug combinations? What symptoms did the individual have? What treatments were received? How did the episodes resolve?

Withdrawal
- **Withdrawal** is the characteristic withdrawal syndrome for the substance. The same (or a closely related) substance may be taken to relieve or avoid withdrawal symptoms.

- Describe withdrawal symptoms or syndromes the patient has ever experienced. What is the pattern of withdrawal symptoms? What relieves the symptoms (e.g., more of the drug and/or a cross-tolerant drug)? Describe the characteristics of withdrawal episodes over time.

- What signs of opioid withdrawal occurred after discontinuation of use (e.g., dysphoria, nausea or vomiting, aching muscles, tearing, rhinorrhea, dilated pupils, piloerection, sweating, diarrhea, yawning, fever, and insomnia)?

- What treatments for withdrawal or its complications have been received in the past?

- **Withdrawal complications.** Is there any history of withdrawal complications (e.g., seizures from withdrawal with sedative-hypnotics or intoxication with stimulants or opioids, delirium tremens, hallucinations)? What treatment was received for these past complications, and what was the treatment response?

Relapse or Attempts at Abstinence

- Has the patient had a persistent desire or made unsuccessful efforts to cut down or control substance use? How many times has the patient attempted to become abstinent? How was the patient able to achieve abstinence? Quantify the longest time completely abstinent from all psychoactive drugs. What was going on during the time of abstinence? To what does the patient attribute his or her abstinence?

- What is the patient's relapse history? What happened to end any abstinent periods? What triggered or preceded relapses? What drug(s) did the patient use when relapsing? What pattern of use developed after the relapses? How did the patient's use patterns change over time with each relapse? Are there any life circumstances that would give clues to events precipitating either relapse or abstinence?

- Has the patient ever been abstinent from all psychoactive drugs for an extended period of time? When and for how long? What has been the longest time free of opioids in the past year, the past 5 years, and lifetime? What has been the longest time free of all psychoactive substances in the past year, the past 5 years, and lifetime? Has the patient switched from one addicting substance to another over time?

Treatment History—Addiction Treatment History

- What previous diagnoses addiction, psychiatric, and medical have been given to this patient?

- Describe all past attempts at detoxification. How many times has detoxification been tried? Was detoxification medically supervised? If so, how long were the detoxification treatments? What were the complications of detoxification? What were the outcomes? How long after detoxification did the patient start using opioids again? Why?

- If the patient has ever been treated for addiction:

  - How many times has he or she received treatment? How long was each treatment?

  - What level(s) of care were received (detoxification, inpatient, residential, outpatient, sober -living environment, and opioid maintenance therapy)? What treatments were received (group, individual, or family psychotherapy; relapse prevention; pharmacotherapy; education; cognitive -behavioral therapy; motivational enhancement therapy; others)? Was the focus of the treatment on psychiatric symptoms or addiction problems, or did the individual receive integrated addiction and psychiatric treatment services? How long was each treatment? Did the patient complete the recommended treatments? If not, why not?

–   Has the patient received pharmacotherapy for addiction? What previous treatment was received (e.g., brief medical detoxification, opioid maintenance therapy, disulfiram, naltrexone, or other medication therapy)? Has previous treatment been medical therapy alone or medical therapy in combination with comprehensive treatment interventions?

–   Was the patient compliant with previous drug and alcohol treatment, including prior opioid treatment programs? Did he or she use drugs and alcohol while in treatment? How long did she remain completely abstinent from all nonprescribed psychoactive drugs after each treatment? Which treatment was the most successful? Which one was least successful? What factors contributed to the success or failure of treatments?

–   Has the patient had contact with Alcoholics Anonymous (AA), Narcotics Anonymous (NA), Cocaine Anonymous (CA), or other 12 Step recovery programs? Ask the patient to describe his or her involvement in those programs. How many meetings were attended? Did he or she ever get a sponsor and work the steps? Does he or she have a current sponsor? How frequent is meeting attendance now?

   – Has the patient been involved in support groups other than 12 Step? If so, which ones? Ask the patient to describe the support groups and the level of his or her activities and involvement.

Psychiatric History

- Review of symptoms: What psychiatric symptoms has the patient ever experienced? Ask about depression, anxiety, irritability, agitation, delusions, hallucinations, mood swings, suicidal thoughts or attempts, homicidal thoughts or attempts, sleep disturbance, appetite or energy disturbance, memory loss, dissociation, etc. What current psychiatric complaints or symptoms does the patient have? Are they related to current drug use or inability to stop using?

- Were psychiatric symptoms present before, during, and/or after substance use? What effects did abstinence from other drugs and alcohol and/or compliance with maintenance treatment have on psychiatric symptoms? Has the patient ever had a substance -induced psychotic disorder, mood disorder, anxiety disorder, persisting perceptual disorder, persisting amnestic disorder, persisting dementia, or sexual dysfunction?

- Has the patient ever had contact with psychiatrists or psychologists? What were previous psychiatric diagnoses? What medications were provided?

- Has the patient ever been in psychotherapy? If so, what kind and for how long? Has he or she ever been hospitalized for psychiatric treatment? If so, what precipitated hospitalization?

- What psychotropic medications have been prescribed and what was the response to each? List current psychotropic medications, prescribers of each medication, and the patient's clinical response.

- Were other treatments recommended? Was the patient compliant? What has helped the most?

- What stressors and traumas have occurred throughout life? Was the patient ever physically, emotionally, and/or sexually abused, or traumatized in other ways? If so, at what age and under what circumstances? Has the patient ever discussed such trauma with a treatment provider or received treatment for these problems?

Family History

- Which biological relatives have a history of addiction, alcoholism, "drinking problems," "drug problems" (including prescription drug addiction), cirrhosis or other associated medical problems, depression, anxiety, sleep problems, attempted or completed suicide or homicide, psychiatric disorders or problems, overdoses, incarceration, criminal involvement, etc.? Have any family members been in recovery from addiction?

- What other illnesses have affected the patient's biological relatives?

Medical History

- Perform a detailed review of systems. What medical problems or complaints does the patient have now? Which ones are or could be related to drug or alcohol use?

- Past medical history: Ask about delirium tremens (DTs), withdrawal complications, or overdoses; tuberculosis or positive purified protein derivative (PPD) skin test, HIV infection, viral hepatitis (hepatitis A, B, C, D), syphilis, gonorrhea, pelvic inflammatory disease, or other sexually transmitted diseases (STDs); menstrual abnormalities, pregnancy or obstetric complications, spontaneous abortion; diabetes, thyroid disease, or other endocrine problem; cancer; hypertension, endocarditis, pericarditis, cardiomyopathy, congestive heart failure, ischemic heart disease, arrhythmia, heart murmur, mycotic aneurysm, thrombophlebitis; gastritis, ulcers, pancreatitis, hepatomegaly, hepatitis, or cirrhosis; pulmonary edema, chronic cough, pneumonia, lung abscess, chronic obstructive pulmonary disease; renal failure, renal calculi; sexual dysfunction; anemia, thrombocytopenia, neutropenia, lymphocytosis, or other blood disorders; lymphadenopathy; aseptic necrosis; osteoporosis; cellulitis, septic arthritis, osteomyelitis; brain, epidural, or subdural abscess; fungal meningitis; other infections; headaches, seizures, stroke, neuropathy, or other neurologic problems; physical trauma, accidents, and hospitalizations; any other medical complications of addiction.

- For any female patient, is it possible that she is pregnant? When was her last menstrual period? Is she sexually active with men? What method of birth control does she use? Does she desire to become pregnant in the near future?

- Obtain the names and addresses of all other physicians currently providing care to the patient and obtain written consent to contact all treatment providers. Does the patient have a designated primary care physician? Is he or she being treated by a number of physicians?

- What medications is the patient taking now, and for what reason? Who prescribed the current medications? What has been the response to medication? Ask the patient to list all current medications and complementary or alternative therapies, such as vitamins, minerals, herbs, and supplements.

- Explore the use, past and present, of addicting prescription drugs. What was the pattern of use of prescription drugs? Did the patient take the medications as prescribed, or more than prescribed, or in combination with alcohol or other drugs? Has the patient received prescriptions from several physicians? Has the patient ever "lost" prescriptions in order to obtain new ones, forged or phoned in prescriptions, stolen prescription pads, split prescriptions with others, or otherwise misused prescription medications?

- Does the patient have pain problems? What pain treatments have been tried or recommended? Have opioid medications been prescribed? What was the response to various pain treatments? What is the level of pain now?

Sexual History
- Is the patient sexually active? How many sexual partners does the patient have? How long has he or she been involved with his or her current partner(s)? Quantify the number and gender of sexual partners over the patient's lifetime. Has the patient had sex with multiple partners or strangers? Has the patient had sex with males, females, or both?

- What specific sexual activities has the patient engaged in? Does he or she ever have sex without a condom or other barrier protection? Has he or she traded sex for money or drugs?

- Has the patient or any of his or her partners ever had or been treated for an STD? If so, which ones (syphilis, gonorrhea, HIV, chlamydia, or others)? How long ago were these treatments? How many times has the patient been treated for an STD?

- Does the patient have any current symptoms of an STD, such as genital discharge, pain, itching, sores, or lumps?

- Has the patient ever been hurt or abused by a sexual partner? Has he or she ever been sexually abused, molested, raped, or assaulted?

- Is sex satisfying for the patient? Does he or she have any problems with or concerns about his or her sexual activities or function?

Cost/Consequences of Drug Use

- What is the patient's current level of functioning in social, family or relationship, educational, occupational, legal, physical health, and mental health arenas?

- Has functioning been affected by drug use? If so, how? What financial, familial, social, emotional, occupational, legal, medical, or spiritual problems have occurred while the patient has been using drugs or as a result of having used drugs? Has the patient experienced legal problems, arrests, been charged with driving while intoxicated, had multiple divorces, marital discord, bankruptcy, fights, injuries, family violence, or suicidal thoughts? Describe specific problems and consequences.

- Has there been hazardous or impairing substance use? If so, describe specifics.

- Has a great deal of time been spent in activities necessary to obtain the substance, use the substance, or recover from its effects? Have important social, occupational, or recreational activities been given up or reduced because of substance use?

- Has there been continued use despite adverse physical and social consequences? Has the substance use continued despite knowledge of having persistent problems that are likely to have been caused or worsened by the substance? If so, give examples.

Compulsivity or Craving

- Does the patient report drug craving and/or urges to use? How does the patient deal with them?

- Does the patient obsess about using drugs? Is there a compulsive pattern to the drug use?

Control

- Has loss of consistent control over drug use occurred? Does the patient feel he or she has ever lost control over use, even one time? When did this first occur? What was the situation? What happened? Has the patient often taken a substance in larger amounts or over a longer period than was intended? Describe the evidence for loss of consistent control over use.

- If the patient does not think control has ever been lost, do others (family, friends, employers, physicians, or others) think differently?

Social and Recovery Environment
- What is the quality of recovery environment for this patient (supportive, nonsupportive, or toxic)? What has been the response of family, significant others, friends, employer, and others to the patient's problems? What is the existing problem as the spouse, partner, or significant other sees it? Have any of these individuals suggested that the patient may have an alcohol or drug problem? When did they first suggest this? What do others object to about the patient's drinking or drug use? What are their concerns or complaints?

- Is the patient's neighborhood, job, or profession a factor that does not support recovery?

- What is or has been the patient's support system? Have supportive individuals been involved in Al-Anon, Nar-Anon, or similar programs? Are they supportive of the patient's getting help? Who has been alienated?

- How many friends, family, or associates are partners in drinking or using? Are alcohol or other drugs present or used in the house where the patient lives? Who is drinking or using drugs in the patient's home? What addicting drugs, either prescribed or nonprescribed, are still at home now?

Insight, Motivation, Readiness to Change
- What is the patient's understanding of his or her problem? What does the patient understand about the disease of addiction?

- What Stage of Change is the patient in now: Precontemplation, Contemplation, Preparation, Action, Maintenance, Relapse? What stages has he or she passed through in the past? How responsive is he or she to motivational enhancement therapy?

Why Now?
- Why did the patient seek treatment or help at this time?

- Is treatment coerced or voluntary? What are the consequences if the patient does not seek help or complete treatment? How does the patient feel about these consequences? [42]

Detection of Drugs in Urine and Other Samples

Some addiction materials expect physicians who use Suboxone for their patients to be super pathologists, with an expertise in urine drug testing. This is an inappropriate expectation and turns off physicians who might want to learn how to use Suboxone. Unfortunately, some addiction groups, trial lawyers, and state medical boards expect physicians to take infinite notes when treating individuals with addictions. This desire for exhaustive documentation is not for the patient or the doctor, but for lawyers and non-clinicians who think that doctors should be scribes. Notes are not as important as connecting with the patient and the notes fetish of these groups should be opposed. Having said this, here are some details about drug screening with the extreme details edited out.

Physicians might try to become familiar with drugs screened in a "routine panel," other specific drug tests, the sensitivity of tests, and the cut off levels for reporting positive or negative test results. A comprehensive discussion of urine drug testing in the primary care setting can be found in *Urine Testing in Primary Care: Dispelling the Myths & Designing Strategies* (http://www.alaskaafp.org/udt.pdf).

Initial screening typically utilizes antigen-antibody interactions and is highly sensitive for specific drugs. Gas chromatography with mass spectrometry (GC/MS) is a highly sensitive and specific test that is labor intensive and costly, and is generally used to confirm the results of screening tests.

Detection of a drug depends on the dose used, frequency of use, last us and characteristics of the specific drug. Most common drugs of abuse, e.g., cocaine, methamphetamine, heroin, marijuana, or their metabolites are readily detectable in the urine. Recent alcohol use is detectable in saliva, breath, blood, and urine samples.

Morphine (the metabolite of heroin) is detected by commercially available urine testing; however, methadone is not detected as an opiate on some drug tests, unless a methadone assay is specifically requested. Oxycodone is only detectable at very high levels. Although buprenorphine and its metabolite are excreted in urine, routine screening for the presence of buprenorphine is not easily available.

Low-potency benzodiazepines (e.g., diazepam and chlordiazepoxide) are readily detected in routine urine drug screens. However, clonazepam, flunitrazepam, alprazolam, and several other benzodiazepines may be undetected in urine samples. Since the combination of buprenorphine and benzodiazepines can be lethal, physicians **might** consider screening for benzodiazepines not tested in your routine screens. A call to the lab director might educate you on the benzodiazepines missed in your common drug screen. Some think this is standard medicine. I think such testing and exploration is extra ordinary medical care.

Stages of Change [43, 44]

As an important component of effective treatment planning, physicians may find it helpful to determine which stage of change characterizes the patient. There are six stages of change:

Precontemplation—you do not intend to make a change in your substance abuse lifestyle.

Contemplation—when you plan to act on your substance problem in the next six months.

Preparation—you plan on treating your substance problem and have started to ponder a plan.

Action—solid actions that are effective at reducing substance abuse.

Maintenance—a person is stable in recovery and working on relapse prevention.

Relapse—a return to any use of the addictive substance.

Patients can be seen moving along a continuum marked by these stages. Stages of change are clearly linked to a patient's motivation. It may be possible for a physician, friend or therapist to increase motivation, and thus help a patient move from an early stage of change (e.g., contemplation) to a more active and healthy stage (e.g., action).

Sample Suboxone Treatment Agreement/Contracts [45]

Treatment agreements/contracts are often employed in the treatment of addiction to make explicit the expectations regarding patient cooperation and involvement in the treatment process. On the following pages are sample addiction treatment agreement/contracts that may be a useful tools in working with patients in an office-based setting.

Suboxone Treatment Contract-Short

As a participant in a buprenorphine protocol for the treatment of opioid abuse and dependence, I freely and voluntarily agree to accept this treatment agreement/contract, as follows:

I agree to keep, and be on time for, all my scheduled appointments with the doctor and his/her assistant.

I agree to conduct myself in a courteous manner in the physician's office.

I agree not to arrive at the office intoxicated or under the influence of drugs. If I do, the doctor will not see me, and I will not be given any medication until my next scheduled appointment.

I agree not to sell, share, or give any of my medication to another individual. I understand that such mishandling of my medication is a serious violation of this agreement and would result in my treatment being terminated without recourse for appeal.

I agree not to deal, steal, or conduct any other illegal or disruptive activities in the doctor's office.

I agree that my medication (or prescriptions) can be given to me only at my regular office visits. Any missed office visits will result in my not being able to get medication until the next scheduled visit.

I agree that the medication I receive is my responsibility and that I will keep it in a safe, secure place. I agree that lost medication will not be replaced regardless of the reasons for such loss.

I agree not to obtain medications from any physicians, pharmacies, or other sources without informing my treating physician. I understand that mixing buprenorphine with other medications, especially benzodiazepines such as Valium, Klonopin, Xanax and other drugs of abuse, can be dangerous. I also understand that a number of deaths have been reported among individuals mixing buprenorphine with benzodiazepines and/or alcohol.

I agree to take my medication as the doctor has instructed and not to alter the dose of my medication without first consulting the doctor.

I understand that medication alone is not sufficient treatment for my disease, and I agree to participate in patient education and relapse prevention programs to assist me in my treatment.

Printed Name_____

Signature_____

Date _____

Suboxone Informed Consent Contract-Expanded

It is good medical practice to provide you with basic information relating to a treatment. Therefore, below are important educational lessons about Suboxone. This informed consent also provides things you must do or you must not do. Please read this information below carefully. If you agree to take Suboxone, it will be assumed you have read this very carefully.

* Suboxone® is approved in the US to treat opioid addiction. It is not the only treatment for opiate addiction. Other treatments include methadone, naltrexone, clonidine and

substance abuse counseling, relapse prevention groups and self-help meetings.

* Buprenorphine is the active medication in Suboxone. Some patients take it for a brief time to detox themselves from an opioid, and others take it daily for months or years to prevent opioid cravings. Suboxone is for people who are dependent on any type of opioid, such as Percocet, oxyco-done, Dilaudid or methadone.

* You cannot start Suboxone while you are still taking your current opioid. If you try to mix Suboxone and your opioid of dependence, you will have a sudden withdrawal.

* Most physicians suggest you not work your first day on Suboxone. You should have close contact with your doctor your first two days on Suboxone. You should not drive your first day on Suboxone in case you are sedated from it.

* If you relapse and use an opioid in addition to Suboxone, please inform your physician, since this information is important to determine future doses and their timing. If you try to get "high" by using high dose opioids while on Suboxone, you could die of an overdose.

* Suboxone combined with any sedating medications carry's a risk or death. Combining Suboxone with alcohol or other sedating medications is dangerous. The combination of buprenorphine with anti-anxiety medications has caused deaths. Examples of these types of medications include Xanax, Ativan, Klonopin, Valium and Serax.

* The liver metabolizes Suboxone. Therefore Suboxone has some liver risk. If you have liver disease the liver side effects are greater. Suboxone interacts with many medications so your physician should be given an accurate list of all your medications and the exact doses. Your physician can make an informed suggestion on interactions with other medications, but adjusting some medications to get the perfect dose will be quite hard and take some time.

* Suboxone is buprenorphine with a small dose of Naloxone. The latter blocks opioid affects and is not really present unless the medication is used IV. Suboxone does create a dependence that is both psychological and physical. Therefore, if you suddenly run out of your medication you will have some withdrawal feelings.

* The initial dose of Suboxone is usually 2 mg. Take it under your tongue and hold it there until it is gone. If you swallow it you will have zero to minimal benefit.

* Currently, many physicians use a variety of dosing. You agree to take the dose discussed and approved by your physician. If you have any pain condition that is **not** related to withdrawal, you might be allowed to try taking your medication three times a day. Patients being treated for simple opioid dependence take Suboxone 1-2 times a day. Discuss your dosing with your doctor.

* **There is no accepted proven conversion table that matches oxycodone or methadone to an exact amount of Suboxone.** Some think 30 mg of methadone is equal to 16 mg per day of Suboxone. This is merely hypothetical thinking and your dose will have to be tailored exactly to you. Some patients do very well on low doses.

After you are in mild withdrawals (at least moderate withdrawals for methadone) you will take 2 mg of Suboxone and then repeat that dose at your physician's direction. You should feel relief with the Suboxone. If you do not, you typically will take repeated doses with your physician's direction until your withdrawal feelings subside. You will adjust your dose to the ideal levels over the next few days to weeks.

* Patients coming from methadone clinics will need to provide a release of information to allow your Suboxone physician to coordinate a **very slow** decrease in your methadone to 30mg per day for a week. You cannot take Suboxone until you have been off methadone for 24-36 hours, since it remains in the blood so long.

* You agree you are being treated according to your wish to be treated. You believe you have been educated sufficiently to understand the treatment. No questions have been left unanswered. You believe Suboxone is in your best interest.

Here is a list of the key points and agreements required for you to successfully work with a Suboxone physician.

1. Buprenorphine treatment is not meant to be a "pill only" treatment. The best treatment for opioid addiction includes substance abuse counseling, 12 step communities or some type of solid support group with addiction experience. I agree to seek special addiction counseling and to learn non-medical ways to promote recovery.

2. The day I start buprenorphine I will not take any opiate for the prior 18-24 hours, e.g., codeine, Dilaudid or

oxycodone. Patients with no signs of opiate withdrawal cannot be started on Suboxone and will be delayed a day or until they have clear withdrawal signs.

3. Do not start your first dose without clear medical direction. It will be 1-4 mg. After 1-3 hours, you will probably be administered an additional dose. The follow up doses for that day will be determined by your response and stability.

4. I will never share my medication.

5. I will never place my Suboxone in another medicine bottle.

6. I had been informed that overdose deaths have occurred with Suboxone's main ingredient, particularly with alcohol, benzodiazepines like Ativan and Klonopin or sedating seizure medications.

7. My physician has permission to coordinate my medication transition from methadone to Suboxone. I understand this will involve a sharing of medical records and possible coordination with the prescribing methadone physician or staff.

8. Once I am on Suboxone I will not take methadone. If I am having methadone or heroin cravings on Suboxone, I will inform my doctor.

9. I agree to keep my appointments on time.

10. I will report my medications honestly and fully.

11. If I relapse, I will inform my doctor honestly.

12. If I am taking any street substances, I will inform my doctors honestly.

13. If I am pregnant or might be pregnant I will tell my physician immediately and make an appointment immediately with an obstetrician. I understand Suboxone is **not** the current standard of care during a pregnancy.

14. I agree to have lab testing to test for my liver health and for drugs of abuse when my physician requests such testing. I will not delay this testing, but will make it a priority.

15. If I have evidence of hepatitis such as yellowing of the eyes or skin, I will report this to my physician.

16. It you take Suboxone regularly it will lead to physical dependence. Therefore, if it is abruptly stopped after a period of regular use, you may experience opioid withdrawal symptoms.

17. Suboxone may provide a transient and modest "high," especially in early use. Therefore, you must protect your personal prescriptions from theft. Some individuals such as roommates, "friends" or relatives might want to steal, "try out," use or sell your Suboxone. Therefore, it must be locked and placed in a location that prevents this from happening.

18. If your Suboxone is lost or stolen, you agree to complete a police report.

19. I fully understand the only way to take Suboxone is to place it under my tongue until it is fully dissolved and absorbed. I will never take Suboxone IV (injected).

20. I understand injecting Suboxone could lead to an immediate and severe opiate withdrawal.

21. I agree that if any person other than me swallows my Suboxone pills, I will call 911 or Poison Control at 1-800-222-1222 immediately.

22. If a pet swallows my Suboxone pills, I will take the pet for an emergency veterinary evaluation.

23. I will carefully store my prescription supplies of Suboxone safely, where it cannot be taken accidentally by children or pets, or stolen by unauthorized users.

24. I understand fully that if my Suboxone is lost or stolen, that my physician will not be able to provide me with make-up prescriptions. Therefore you may experience Suboxone withdrawal.

25. If my Suboxone is stolen, I understand completely that I will have to report this to the police. The police will complete a report, and I will bring a copy of this police report to my physician before I am given another Suboxone prescription.

26. I will bring my bottle of Suboxone in with me for every appointment.

27. If my Suboxone is damaged, e.g., by being placed in the washing machine, you will bring the bottle to the physician for evaluation and may be asked to get a toxicology screen.

28. I understand that Suboxone is approved by the Food and Drug Administration for treating opioid dependence.

29. In understand my physician can only treat thirty people with Suboxone at a time.

30. If my Suboxone is suddenly stopped I may experience muscle aches, stomach cramps, nausea, or diarrhea lasting days.

31. I understand Suboxone should be stopped slowly over several weeks or months.

32. Combining buprenorphine with alcohol or some other medications may be dangerous.

33. You agree to treat the office staff and the physician reasonably and with respect.

34. You agree never to verbally insult or abuse a pharmacist or pharmacy employee. They do not have to stock Suboxone, and it is an extra headache for them to do so. If they make a mistake or do not handle your prescription correctly, you agree not to take out your frustration in any verbally hostile manner. Discuss the problem with your physician.

35. You understand any swallowed Suboxone tablet is functionally lost. You must hold the tablet under your tongue until dissolved, and then the medication is absorbed over 15 minutes to two hours.

36. Suboxone interacts with many medications, especially HIV and seizure medications. This book lists a large number of common medications altered by Suboxone. But no medication interaction list is entirely complete.

37. You agree to pay your medical fees at the time services are rendered unless a prior arrangement has been made.

38. I have been informed of many alternatives to Suboxone. Some other sample treatment options I have besides Suboxone include: hospitals with special drug abuse treatment units, special hospital detoxification units and/or residential drug abuse counseling centers. I am also aware of out-patient treatment centers and counselors who offer individual one-on-one counseling and group therapy. Other forms of opioid treatment include daily methadone treatment or naltrexone that prevents any opioid used during a "slip" or relapse from making you "high."

39. I understand my physician's office hours, emergency procedures, office phone numbers, how to make an appointment and the fee policies.

40. I will not drive my first three days on Suboxone. I will not risk possible Suboxone sedation while driving.

41. I am not currently pregnant, and I will not attempt to become pregnant. If I have sex I will use two forms of birth control.

42. I understand the safety of buprenorphine during pregnancy is not known.

43. It is clear to me that the use of sedative medications such as Valium, Ativan, Xanax, Klonopin or any other benzodiazepine drug, could be so serious as to result in an **accidental overdose, dangerous sedation, coma, or death.**

44. You understand your physician will expect you to look into weaning yourself from the addiction of all illegal or harmful drugs.

45. I understand my active addiction to drugs can benefit from both individual and group counseling.

46. I agree that I will be open and honest with my counselors and physician about cravings, relapse fantasies or a relapse before a drug test result shows it.

47. I agree that solid and effective substance abuse recovery requires a "team." Therefore I freely give permission to my doctor or other staff parties to be in contact with my closest relatives, friends, therapists, probation officers and parole officers.

48. I agree to not adjust my Suboxone dose on my own. If I wish to change my dose, I will call the office for an appointment to discuss this, and my physician can change the dose.

49. It has been explained to me that buprenorphine itself is an opiate drug that can produce physical dependence that is similar to heroin.

50. I understand I can continue Suboxone as long as necessary to prevent relapse to opiate abuse.

51. I accept periodic testing for drugs of abuse is to detect early relapse and to document my progress in treatment. Initially, it may be done weekly and may be decreased in frequency as I progress in treatment.

52. Buprenorphine will be prescribed in quantities to last from visit to visit. The frequency of visits depends on how I am progressing.

53. Lost prescriptions or lost buprenorphine tablets are a serious issue and may result in discontinuation of buprenorphine therapy from this office.

54. I agree to tell my physician if I become pregnant or even think I may be pregnant. If you are not using two forms of birth control, you are open to the risk of pregnancy. Suboxone's safety to a fetus cannot be guaranteed, and it may cause birth defects in some.

55. Be aware that hundreds of medications interact with birth control pills and can make them less effective. This is not commonly known. Therefore, this issue of birth control pill interaction must be asked explicitly of any physician offering you a new prescription. If you are able, search for drug interactions on your computer by placing the drug name in the search bar with the word "interactions."

56. Suboxone has the potential to cause you to be sleepy or sedated during the first days of use or if you are given too much. You agree never to drive a motor vehicle, work on heights, walk on high stairs, use ladders, climb on roofs, use power tools or other dangerous machinery during your first days of taking Suboxone,

or at any time in which you feel sedated, to make sure you do not hurt yourself or others as a side-effect of taking Suboxone.

I have read and understand fully each and every point in the pages above about Suboxone. I wish to be treated with Suboxone. I have not simply signed this form impulsively, but agree to understand and *read each point in full before ever starting Suboxone.*

Patient signature: _____ Date: _____

Patient printed name: _____

Witness getting consent: _____ Date: _____

Benzodiazepine Treatment Contract [46]

I freely and voluntarily agree to accept this treatment contract, as follows:

1. I agree that the medication I receive is my responsibility and I will keep it in a very safe and secure place. I understand that it is a felony to keep a benzodiazepine outside its properly labeled container as it is a controlled substance under the Controlled Substances Act 1970 21 U.S.C. §801 et seq. & sec 1308 Title 21 (CFR) Part 1300. I understand that these medications have a limited abuse liability, but that in my case, I may be at increased risk of abusing these medications.

2. If I loose my medication, I agree that the medication will not be replaced regardless of the reasons for such loss. It is my physician's responsibility to prohibit abuse of these medications.

I understand that these medications may cause very serious withdrawal symptoms including seizures, panic attacks, hallucinations and psychosis if stopped suddenly. If I experience any of these problems I will go to the nearest emergency room.

3. I agree that my medication or prescriptions can only be given to me at my regular office visits. Any missed office visits will result in my not being able to get medication until the next scheduled visit. Further, I agree not to obtain medications from any physicians, pharmacies, or other sources without informing my treating physician. Doing so may constitute fraud, a felony punishable by prison sentence.

4. I understand that mixing benzodiazepines, such as Valium, Xanax, Ativan, Klonopin with alcohol or other drugs can be dangerous if not fatal. I understand that thousands of deaths have occurred among persons mixing benzodiazepine tranquilizers with alcohol, opioid narcotics and other drugs.

5. I agree to take my medication as my doctor has instructed, and not to alter the way I take my medication without first consulting my doctor. I agree not to exceed a daily dose of _____ unless expressly authorized by my doctor beforehand.

   My use of these medications will be supervised by _____.

6. I understand that medication alone may not be sufficient treatment for my disease and I agree to participate in any patient education or Relapse Prevention program, as discussed, to assist me in my treatment and recovery.

7. I agree not to sell, share or give any of my medication to another person.

8. I agree to keep all my scheduled appointments with the doctor.

_____   _____
Patient's signature   Witness signature

_____   _____
Date   Date

Who Is Qualified to Prescribe Suboxone?

A physician can take a 8-9 hour training course from any of the following sources listed below, and then can prescribe it with a second special DEA number which is sent to them after they file a simple application.

Information about a wide range of SUBOXONE training courses can be found at:

* DocOptIn.com

* American Academy of Addiction Psychiatry (AAAP)
  Phone: (202) 393-4484
  Contact: www.aaap.org/contact.htm
  Website: www.aaap.org

* American Osteopathic Academy of
  Addiction Medicine (AOAAM)
  Phone: (800) 621-1773
  Website: www.aoaam.org

* American Psychiatric Association (APA)
  Phone: (703) 907-7300
  E-mail: apa@psych.org
  Website: www.psych.org

* American Society of Addiction Medicine (ASAM)
  Phone: (301) 656-3920
  E-mail: email@asam.org
  Website: www.asam.org

Some of the above organizations also offer CD and Internet training that counts as part or all of the required 8 hours to be certified.

However, some physicians are believed qualified to use Suboxone by virtue of their training. These individuals include physicians with:

- an addiction psychiatry subspecialty board certification
- addiction medicine certification from ASAM
- an addiction medicine subspecialty board certification (for DO's)
- an investigator in trials leading to Suboxone approval
- special approval by a state board based on experience
- special approval by the United States Secretary of Health and Human Services based on experience

Also, currently physicians are asked to have *referral options for services they cannot provide in the treatment of opioid addiction.* I would add that if a person has medical issues like HIV, TB or other complex medical issues, that they be referred to therapists and physicians who can help them. If you are in a remote location, just do your best, but try not to imagine a person's entire life is fixed with one pill.

I personally would suggest taking a Suboxone course no matter what your medical training, especially since it can be done so many ways at home or at many local settings. Suboxone really is a unique drug and we are continuing to learn new interesting information about it.

New Forms of Suboxone

In future editions of this book, I will be discussing new delivery options for people who use Suboxone. Currently many versions are being researched or are in other countries. These include pellets placed just under the skin that release a long term and steady amount of the medication. Transdermal patches and creams are also being explored. New types of very long acting "depot" injections might be available in the future in which the medication lasts for a highly extended period of time.

Suboxone and Benzodiazapines (Anti-anxiety Agents)

We know that some addicted persons in France have taken IV buprenorphine and IV benzodiazepines and died. Obviously IV is a powerful route that bypasses the liver's ability to remove a large portion or a drug. IV routes also release a medication very quickly. Yet some consent forms say you should never be given a benzodiazepine—even if orally and even if other treatments I have discussed above have failed.

I have successfully used oral modestly dosed benzodiazepines like Ativan, Klonopin, Serax, Valium and Xanax to treat panic attacks, generalized anxiety and social phobia in many individuals. Earlier in this book, I have discussed the options one should generally try before using benzodiazepines. Also, I will **not** use them in alcoholics, because modest drinking, oral benzodiazepines and Suboxone could cause death. It is unknown how easily this could happen, but I do not want to find out.

The Case for Benzodiazapines in Medicine

Some very sincere addictionologists have seen individuals abuse anti-anxiety medications and do dangerous things while on them. This has lead to a concern that they should never be used. I appreciate their fear, but the other side of this argument is some patients are not successful with cognitive behavioral anxiety therapy or other medications to treat crippling anxiety. Also, many of these writers confuse normal feelings with pathological anxiety. I have even met veteran addictionologists who oppose benzodiazepines with obvious anxiety disorders that are going untreated.

Ted was a senior official at a huge multi-national company in his late 30's. He was crippled with agony if anyone looked at him over thirty seconds. He was even shy around his own employees. When I met him his hand trembled as I introduced myself and shook his hand.

He was placed on an antidepressant. When that only worked 40%, he was placed on Klonopin 0.5 mg three times a day. He was fully alert. He had abused alcohol for ten years in his 20's prior to our work, because "I could not stand talking to anyone with so much panic." This cost him a possible marriage with the woman of his dreams.

On these two medications he is now the sought after MC and speaker for his entire multi-national corporation. He has become highly regarded for his "humor!" So now a man that was terrified to meet me, is leading events, which have hundreds to thousands of people present.

Since the liver makes enzymes to remove toxins, drugs, herbs and complex food molecules, any stable Klonopin dose will need to be increased twice in the first year. Based on my unpublished research on Zoloft (sertraline) blood levels, we see the same need to increase the dose in Zoloft patients in order to keep the blood level the same. Yet addictionologists rarely are "addicting" patients to Zoloft. This is first grade physiology of the liver. One needs to increase a drug to keep the same blood level in the first year.

Some fear they will become addicted to benzodiazepines. Yes. Your body will get used to this medication in the same way it will get used to Paxil or Effexor. If you suddenly stop the antidepressants Paxil or Effexor you will feel very ill and might require many months to "get off" these medications. But few say you are addicted. Why not?

If a person's anxiety disorder(s) are magically cured you will need to decrease your dose slowly with your physician. We rarely drop it more than 10% every two weeks.

We have had individuals with illnesses that caused inflammation and agitation like Bartonella, Borrelia (Lyme disease) or indoor Aspergillus/Penicillium mold toxin exposure. Once I treated these problems, their panic or other anxiety disorders dissolved over 3-12 months. Then they were able to come off the benzodiazepine because the cause was not simply genetic, but a finite illness.

Sadism and a Lack of Empathy

I had to pay for my three years of graduate school, my 5 1/2 years of college, my medical education and some money to survive. One day I calculated that I would be paying a massive monthly cost for my self-funded education until I was 52. All of a sudden a massive panic hit me, and I was on the floor and could not breathe or move.

I had taught others how to de-escalate panic and reminded myself I was not going to die, I would simply handle this cost as a business expense, and I loved helping folks through medicine. In 7-10 minutes I was OK. Since my thoughts had started the panic attack, I was able to use thoughts to remove it. These techniques might help all people with panic, but often they do not work to remove 100% of the panic. I have seen these treatments oversold to patients. I meet patients who are "cured" by experts and they are obviously still agitated.

I frequently hear patients tell me that they are told they must stop taking benzodiazepines, even when these medications have been highly successful. This can happen when you move and have a new doctor, or your past doctor retires, or your insurance is changed and you have to go to a new family doctor or a new psychiatrist.

Further, some suffering individuals have never been offered benzodi-azepines, because the physician fears the DEA, some ignorant state medical board lawyers and physicians, opinionated pharmacists or opinionated relatives who warn of "addiction." If these folks were given IV chemicals that cause panic attacks, they would quickly change their tune after the first five panic attacks.

While some patients need dose increases in the first year, some studies show many patients with anxiety disorders lower their dose over time.

Patients taking benzodiazepines over 4 weeks can develop some physical dependence. So if someone stops their benzodiazepine abruptly, withdrawal symptoms might begin. This is why it is best to stop your benzodiazepines under the guidance of your physician with a gradual taper.

I strongly suggest you see a psychiatrist who specializes in anxiety disorders and who is a pharmacologist, or someone who really knows psychiatric medications. Most family doctors do not have the expertise or the training to understand benzodiazepines, and you need at least 30-45 minutes to be taught about them.

It is possible if you are taking a benzodiazepine and suddenly stop it, you might have a seizure. I have never seen this, but one of my friends who is an emergency room physician has seen it once.

If you have to raise your dose every couple weeks or months repeatedly, you might be ill with something that is easily missed like hyperthyroidism, Bartonella, Borrelia (Lyme disease) or indoor Aspergillus/Penicillium mold toxin exposure. Or you might have an addiction problem. Perhaps you are better off on low dose Seroquel such as 6-12 mg at night before bed as a trial.

Some key quotes on the issue of benzodiazepines:

1. "With panic/agoraphobia patients there is no evidence of abuse. Chronic use is justified in these patients... There is no epidemic of misuse." [47]

2. "The vast majority of the use of benzodiazepines is appropriate." [48]

3. "In [people with substance abuse histories] ... benzodiazepines almost never induce behavior that satisfies
any reasonable definition of addiction" [49]

Some Sincere People Just
Do Not Understand Biological Anxiety

I once took a man to an AA meeting. His labs were so bad; it was
obvious he had significant blood inflammation, which was causing
intense anxiety. At the AA meeting he was told he was a "cheat" and
an "addict" because he was on Klonopin for panic. The only thing
that allowed him to come to a strange new place like this meeting
was the Klonopin.

The "Masking the Real Problem" Argument

While some people have deep emotional wounds from abuse, excess
stress, and various fears, which could be helped by a caring therapeu-
tic group and/or therapist, for many people this will not be a cure.

Some naive people do not understand that their psychobabble is from
the 1950's, and they have a person's anxiety cause reversed. Simply,
anxious feelings are **the sign the biological anxiety centers of the
brain are being agitated and stirred up.** Some folks approach patients on anti-anxiety medication in abusive and insulting ways.

Some uneducated people call a person with deep heartache "flawed"
and in need of "addressing their covered up deep emotions," as the
person is dying of a heart attack. Sometimes you can go no deep-
er than the biology—that is the deepest part. Of course sometimes
psychology or meaning influences physiology or panic. If this occurs,
many different therapy techniques can be of use. I am trained in
many non-medical anxiety approaches, and they have some real use,
but are often over sold as cures for both anxiety and depression.

In terms of various books and Internet articles talking about benzodiazepine addiction, I have noted most seem obviously written with no understanding of severe anxiety disorders. Anxiety disorders are not "a dash" of "nerves," but are very common genetic illnesses. They are more common that biological depression. Many of these anti-anxiety medication books and web sites show pronounced ignorance of how benzodiazapines work. They often consider that a missed dose with resulting anxiety or a couple increased doses in the first year as signs of severe addiction. By this standard most antidepressants and other medications with zero street value are also addictive. One might also say that an AA or NA meeting is addictive by the same criteria—you miss an AA meeting (a dose) and you are not feeling well, and you feel you have to increase you number of meetings from 5/week to 9/week to improve your health and sense of wholeness. Of course this is nonsense. It is also nonsense when people with no experience with severe anxiety or with an understanding of liver function pathologize benzodiazepines.

Some patients have an increased suicide or relapse risk when they have anxiety that is left untreated. Agitation clearly increases suicide.

So people need to be careful not to assume **their** benzodiazepine addiction is what is happening to others.

Benzodiazepine Safety

There is absolutely no evidence that benzodiazepines cause permanent damage to the brain, nervous system or body. However, the addition of alcohol to benzodiazepines does result in fast sedation and intoxication that could lead to DUI dangers and a risk of falls. Benzodiazapines carry a category D pregnancy risk. Meaning, I would not take them while pregnant. [50]

The American Psychiatric Association, the main expert specialty with experience in treating anxiety, supports the use of benzodiazepines being covered in Medicare's new prescription program, and they have fought specifically to make them available. They report their psychiatrists and patients are grateful for benzodiazepine access. [51]

Glossary of Suboxone Related Words and Laws [52]

21 C.F.R. Part 291
Code of Federal Regulations (C.F.R.) that, among other things, sets standards for narcotic treatment and use of methadone.

42 C.F.R. Part 2
Federal Regulation concerning confidentiality of alcohol and drug abuse patient treatment records.

42 C.F.R. Part 8
Federal Regulation concerning dispensing of drugs through opioid treatment programs.

Addiction
A behavioral syndrome characterized by the repeated, compulsive seeking or use of a substance despite adverse social, psychological, and/or physical consequences. Addiction is often (but not always) accompanied by physical dependence, a withdrawal syndrome, and tolerance.

Alcoholism
A pattern of compulsive use of alcohol in which individuals devote substantial periods of time to obtaining and consuming alcoholic beverages despite adverse psychological or physical consequences, e.g., depression, blackouts, liver disease, or other consequences. (Adapted from *Diagnostic and Statistical Manual of Mental Disorders,* 4th ed., Text Revision [DSM -IV -TR].)

Antagonist
Substance that tends to nullify the effect of another (e.g., a drug that binds to a receptor without eliciting a response).

AUDIT
Alcohol **U**se **D**isorders **I**dentification **T**est. A screening tool for identification of alcohol use disorders.

Biopsychosocial
Combining biological, psychological, and social concerns or effects.

Buprenex® (Generic: buprenorphine)
Injectable formulation of the Schedule III narcotic (opioid) partial agonist buprenorphine. Approved for use as an analgesic. Not approved for use in the treatment of opioid addiction.

Buprenorphine
An opioid partial agonist that is a synthetic derivative of thebaine. Two sublingual formulations of buprenorphine, the Schedule III pharmaceuticals Subutex (buprenorphine) and Suboxone (buprenorphine/naloxone), received Food and Drug Administration (FDA) approval in October 2000 for use in the treatment of opioid addiction. Buprenex , an injectable formulation of buprenorphine, has previously been available in the United States and is approved for use as a parenteral analgesic.

Buprenorphine/naloxone
Drug combination; see separate definitions and brand name Suboxone .

CAGE -AID
CAGE Questionnaire **A**dapted to **I**nclude **D**rugs.

CAGE Questionnaire
A screening tool for identification of alcohol use disorders (questions use words beginning with letters C, A, G, and E consecutively).

Children's Health Act of 2000 (P.L. 106 -310)
Legislation (Public Law) that authorizes expanded research and services for a variety of childhood health problems, reauthorizes programs of the Substance Abuse and Mental Health Services Administration (SAMHSA), addresses the problem of youth substance abuse and the violence associated with it, and works to improve the health and safety of children in child care. Title XXXV of the Children's Health Act is the Drug Addiction Treatment Act of 2000 (DATA

2000), which authorizes qualifying physicians to treat opioid addiction in clinical settings other than the Opioid Treatment Program (OTP) setting.

CINA
Clinical Institute Narcotic Assessment Scale for Withdrawal. An interview and observation tool for assessing opioid withdrawal signs and symptoms.

COWS
Clinical Opiate Withdrawal Scale. An interview and observation tool for assessing opioid withdrawal signs and symptoms.

DAST 10
Drug **A**buse **S**creening **T**est. A questionnaire tool for identification of drug and alcohol use disorders.

DATA 2000
See Drug Addiction Treatment Act of 2000.

Dependence
A condition manifested as a characteristic set of withdrawal signs and symptoms upon reduction, cessation, or loss of the active compound at cell receptors (a withdrawal syndrome).

Drug Addiction Treatment Act of 2000
Title XXXV of the Children's Health Act of 2000. The Drug Addiction Treatment Act of 2000 (DATA 2000) establishes a waiver authority for qualifying physicians to prescribe or dispense specially approved Schedule III, IV, and V narcotic medications for the treatment of opioid addiction in clinical settings other than the Opioid Treatment Program setting.

HIPAA
Health **I**nsurance **P**ortability and **A**ccountability **A**ct.

LAAM

Closely related to methadone, the synthetic compound levo -alpha -acetyl -methadol or LAAM (Brand name: ORLAMM), has an even longer duration of action (from 48 to 72 hours) than methadone, permitting a reduction in frequency of use. In 1994, it was approved as a Schedule II treatment drug for narcotic addiction. Both methadone and LAAM have high abuse potential. Their acceptability as narcotic treatment drugs is predicated on their ability to substitute for heroin, the long duration of action, and their mode of oral administration. [The maker of LAAM has stopped production, perhaps due to cardiac risk concerns].

MAST

Michigan **A**lcohol **S**creening **T**est. A questionnaire tool for identification of alcohol use disorders.

MCV

Mean corpuscular volume.

Methadone

A Schedule II synthetic opioid with pharmacologic actions similar to morphine and heroin; almost equally addictive. Approved for use in the treatment of opioid addiction in federally regulated Opioid Treatment Programs. May be administered orally, intramuscularly, and subcutaneously.

Monotherapy

Therapy using one drug or approach.

Morphine

Most active narcotic alkaloid of opium. Has powerful analgesic action; abuse leads to dependence.

Mu agonist

A drug that has affinity for and stimulates physiologic activity at mu opioid cell receptors. See also opioid full agonist.

Mu opioid receptor
A receptor on the surface of brain cells that mediates opioid analgesia, tolerance, and addiction through drug -induced activation. When an opioid agonist, or partial agonist (e.g., buprenorphine), binds to a mu opioid receptor, a series of other proteins associated with the mu receptor -signalling pathway becomes activated. Other opioid receptors are the delta and kappa receptors.

Naloxone
Brand name: Narcan. An opioid antagonist, similar to naltrexone, that works by blocking opioid receptors in the brain, thereby blocking the effects of opioid full agonists (e.g., heroin, morphine) and partial agonists (e.g., buprenorphine).

Naltrexone
Naltrexone, a narcotic antagonist, works by blocking opioid receptors in the brain and therefore blocking the effects of opioid full agonists (e.g., heroin, morphine) and partial agonists (e.g., buprenorphine).

NATA
Narcotic **A**ddict **T**reatment **A**ct.

Needle embolization
Blood clot caused by use of a needle. If dislodged, the clot may cause death.

Nonopioid
Drug or compound not related to natural or synthetic opium and related alkaloids.

OAT
Opioid **A**gonist **T**reatment.

Opioids
Drugs that are derived naturally from the flower of the opium poppy plant (e.g., morphine and heroin) and those that are synthetically produced in the lab (e.g., methadone and oxycodone).

Used therapeutically to treat pain, they also produce a sensation of euphoria or a "high." Repeated misuse and abuse of opioids often leads to dependence and addiction.

Opioid full agonist
Drugs that have affinity for and stimulate physiologic activity at opioid cell receptors (mu, kappa, and delta) that are normally stimulated by naturally occurring opioids. Repeated administration often leads to dependence and addiction.

Opioid partial agonist
Drugs that can both activate and block opioid receptors, depending on the clinical situation. Partial agonists have properties of both agonists and antagonists. The mu agonist properties of partial agonists reach a maximum at a certain dose and do not continue to increase with increasing doses of the partial agonist. This is termed the ceiling effect. The ceiling effect limits the abuse potential and untoward side effects of opioid partial agonists. The Schedule III medication buprenorphine is an opioid partial agonist.

Parenteral
Not through the gastrointestinal route; for instance, given via intramuscular or intravenous injection.

Pharmacodynamics
Study of the biochemical and physiological effects of drugs and the mechanisms of their actions, including correlation of these actions and effects with the drugs' chemical structure.

Pharmacokinetics
Study of the action of drugs in the body over a period of time, including the processes of absorption, distribution, localization in tissues, biotransformation, and excretion.

Pharmacotherapy
Treatment of disease by using medicines.

Polysubstance abuse
Concurrent use or abuse of multiple substances (e.g., drinking alcohol as well as smoking tobacco, snorting cocaine, inhaling glue fumes).

Psychosocial
Combining psychological and social aspects.

SMAST
Short Michigan Alcohol Screening Test. Shortened, self-administered version of the MAST alcohol use disorder screening tool.

SOWS
Subjective **O**pioid **W**ithdrawal **S**cale. Self-administered scale for grading opioid withdrawal symptoms.

Sublingual
Under the tongue.

Suboxone®
Brand name for the Schedule III sublingual formulation of buprenorphine combined with naloxone. Received FDA approval in October 2000 for use in the treatment of opioid addiction. Naloxone is added to the formulation to decrease the likelihood of abuse of the combination via the parenteral route.

Subutex®
Brand name for the Schedule III sublingual formulation of buprenorphine. Received FDA approval in October 2000 for use in the treatment of opioid addiction.

Talc granulomatosis

Formation of granulomas (small nodules) as a chronic inflammatory response, in the lungs or other organs, in this case to talc or other fine powder. Talc granulomatosis may occur in drug users because many injected drugs have been adulterated with an inert substance (such as talcum powder) to cut or dilute the amount of drug.

Liquid Conversion to Tablet Dosing [53]

Some studies on buprenorphine use liquid forms. If you are trying to understand what this dose is in tablet size, consider using this table for conversion.

2 mg solution would be roughly equivalent to 3 mg tablet
4 mg solution would be roughly equivalent to 6 mg tablet
8 mg solution would be roughly equivalent to 12 mg tablet
16 mg solution would be roughly equivalent to 24 mg tablet

End Notes

1. Rubin R. New drug treats the new face of addiction. *USA TODAY*. 2006. http://www.usatoday.com/news/health/2006-01-23-bupe-treatment_x.htm

2. Rubin R. New drug treats the new face of addiction. *USA TODAY*. 2006. http://www.usatoday.com/news/health/2006-01-23-bupe-treatment_x.htm

3. http://www.naabt.org/documents/VACampanaDrugabusebyFrank-Shatz.doc

4. Bender KJ. Sleeping Through Detox Poses Hazards. *Psychiatric Times*. 2005;23

5. Collins ED, Kleber HD, Whittington RA, Heitler NE. Anesthesia-assisted vs. buprenorphine- or clonidine-assisted heroin detoxification and naltrexone induction: a randomized trial. *JAMA*. 2005; 294:903-913 [see comment].

6. O'Connor PG. Methods of detoxification and their role in treating patients with opioid dependence. *JAMA*. 2005; 294:961-963 [editorial].

7. http://www.medicalnewstoday.com/medicalnews.php?newsid=29619#

8. http://www.medicalnewstoday.com/medicalnews.php?newsid=29619#

9. Graham AW, Schultz TK, Mayo-Smith MF, Reis RK, Wilford BB. *Principles of Addiction Medicine*. 3rd edition. Chevy Chase, Maryland: ASAM, 2003. pg. 657.

10. Cowan A, Lewis J. *Buprenorphine: Combatting Drug Abuse with a Unique Opioid.* 1995;New York: Wiley-Liss, preface xv.

11. Coen A. Update on the general pharmacology of buprenorphine. In Cowan A, Lewis J. *Buprenorphine: Combatting Drug Abuse with a Unique Opioid.* 1995; New York: Wiley-Liss, p. 32.

12. Michael Sheehan, personal communication, March, 2005.

13. Bodkin JA, Zornberg GL, Lukas SE, Cole JO. Buprenorphine treatment of refractory depression. *Journal of Clinical Psychopharmacology.* 1995;15:49-57.

14. Center for Substance Abuse Treatment. *Clinical Guidelines for the Use of Buprenorphine in the Treatment of Opioid Addiction.* Treatment Improvement Protocol (TIP) Series 40. DHHS Publication No. (SMA) 04 -3939. Rockville, MD: Substance Abuse and Mental Health Services Administration, 2004. Page 8. [Title modified]

15. http://www.suboxone.com/hcp/pharmacists/pharmacists_faqs. aspx

16. Center for Substance Abuse Treatment. *Clinical Guidelines for the Use of Buprenorphine in the Treatment of Opioid Addiction.* Treatment Improvement Protocol (TIP) Series 40. DHHS Publication No. (SMA) 04 -3939. Rockville, MD: Substance Abuse and Mental Health Services Administration, 2004. Page 13. [Labeling is modified]

17. Center for Substance Abuse Treatment. *Clinical Guidelines for the Use of Buprenorphine in the Treatment of Opioid Addiction.* Treatment Improvement Protocol (TIP) Series 40. DHHS Publication No. (SMA) 04 -3939. Rockville, MD: Substance Abuse and Mental Health Services Administration, 2004. Page 32. [Slightly modified and simplified].

18. Wesson DR, Ling W. The Clinical Opiate Withdrawal Scale (COWS). *J Psychoactive Drugs.* 2003;35:253-9. Reprinted with permission.

19. Rossi S, editor. *Australian Medicines Handbook.* 2005. Adelaide: Australian Medicines Handbook.

20. Brown RL, Rounds LA. Conjoint screening questionnaires for alcohol and other drug abuse: Criterion validity in a primary care practice. *Wisconsin Medical Journal.* 1995;94:135-140.

21. http://www.rxlist.com/cgi/generic3/suboxone_wcp.htm

22. Rossi S, editor. *Australian Medicines Handbook.* 2005. Adelaide: Australian Medicines Handbook.

23. Center for Substance Abuse Treatment. *Clinical Guidelines for the Use of Buprenorphine in the Treatment of Opioid Addiction.* Treatment Improvement Protocol (TIP) Series 40. DHHS Publication No. (SMA) 04 -3939. Rockville, MD: Substance Abuse and Mental Health Services Administration, 2004. Page 75.

24. Reprinted with written permission from M. Sheehan. Some material from: Center for Substance Abuse Treatment. *Clinical Guidelines for the Use of Buprenorphine in the Treatment of Opioid Addiction.* Treatment Improvement Protocol (TIP) Series 40. DHHS Publication No. (SMA) 04 -3939. Rockville, MD: Substance Abuse and Mental Health Services Administration, 2004. Page 148.

25. http://www.aatod.org/print_version/print_drug_court.html

26. Center for Substance Abuse Treatment. *Clinical Guidelines for the Use of Buprenorphine in the Treatment of Opioid Addiction.* Treatment Improvement Protocol (TIP) Series 40. DHHS Publication No. (SMA) 04 -3939. Rockville, MD: Substance Abuse and Mental Health Services Administration, 2004.

27. Graham AW, Schultz TK, Mayo-Smith MF, Reis RK, Wilford BB. *Principles of Addiction Medicine.* 3rd edition. Chevy Chase, Maryland: ASAM, 2003. pg. 657.

28. M. Sheehan, personal correspondence March 27, 2006.

29. Pirastu R., Fais R, Messina M, Bini V, Falconieri D, Diana M. Impaired decision making in opiate-dependent subjects: Effect of pharmacological therapies. *Drug Alcohol Depend.* 2005. Dec 9. [Epub ahead of print].

30. Krantz MJ, Garcia JA, Mehler PS. Effects of buprenorphine on cardiac repolarization in a patient with methadone-related torsade de pointes. *Pharmacotherapy.* 2005;25:611-4.

31. Bliesener N, Albrecht S, Schwager A, Weckbecker K, Lichtermann D, Klingmuller D. *J Clin Endocrinol Metab.* 2005; 90:203-6.

32. Rossi S, editor. *Australian Medicines Handbook.* 2005. Adelaide: Australian Medicines Handbook.

33. http://www.suboxone.com/hcp/pharmacists/pharmacists_faqs. aspx [Modified for clarity and simplicity]

34. Center for Substance Abuse Treatment. *Clinical Guidelines for the Use of Buprenorphine in the Treatment of Opioid Addiction.* Treatment Improvement Protocol (TIP) Series 40. DHHS Publication No. (SMA) 04 -3939. Rockville, MD: Substance Abuse and Mental Health Services Administration, 2004. Page 76.

35. http://www.rxpgnews.com/research/psychiatry/substancemisuse/ opiates/article_2565.shtml

36. Marsch LA, Bickel WK, Badger GJ, Stothart ME, Quesnel KJ, Stanger C, Brooklyn J. Comparison of pharmacological treatments for opioid-dependent adolescents: a randomized controlled trial. *Archives of General Psychiatry.* 2005;62:1165.

37. Center for Substance Abuse Treatment. *Clinical Guidelines for the Use of Buprenorphine in the Treatment of Opioid Addiction.* Treatment Improvement Protocol (TIP) Series 40. DHHS Publication No. (SMA) 04 -3939. Rockville, MD: Substance Abuse and Mental Health Services Administration, 2004. Page 21.

38. Center for Substance Abuse Treatment. *Clinical Guidelines for the Use of Buprenorphine in the Treatment of Opioid Addiction.* Treatment Improvement Protocol (TIP) Series 40. DHHS Publication No. (SMA) 04 -3939. Rockville, MD: Substance Abuse and Mental Health Services Administration, 2004. Page 30. [Some words modified and bolding added for simplicity]

39. Center for Substance Abuse Treatment. *Clinical Guidelines for the Use of Buprenorphine in the Treatment of Opioid Addiction.* Treatment Improvement Protocol (TIP) Series 40. DHHS Publication No. (SMA) 04 -3939. Rockville, MD: Substance Abuse and Mental Health Services Administration, 2004. Page 34.

40. Center for Substance Abuse Treatment. *Clinical Guidelines for the Use of Buprenorphine in the Treatment of Opioid Addiction.* Treatment Improvement Protocol (TIP) Series 40. DHHS Publication No. (SMA) 04 -3939. Rockville, MD: Substance Abuse and Mental Health Services Administration, 2004. Page 44 [Modified partly for clarity and functionality].

41. Center for Substance Abuse Treatment. *Clinical Guidelines for the Use of Buprenorphine in the Treatment of Opioid Addiction.* Treatment Improvement Protocol (TIP) Series 40. DHHS Publication No. (SMA) 04 -3939. Rockville, MD: Substance Abuse and Mental Health Services Administration, 2004. Page 41.

42. Center for Substance Abuse Treatment. *Clinical Guidelines for the Use of Buprenorphine in the Treatment of Opioid Addiction.* Treatment Improvement Protocol (TIP) Series 40. DHHS Publication No. (SMA) 04 -3939. Rockville, MD: Substance Abuse and Mental Health Services Administration, 2004. Page 122-128 [Enlarge fonts for easier reading].

43. The discussion of Stages of Changes is found in *Enhancing Motivation for Change in Substance Abuse Treatment.* Tip 35. DHHS Publication No. BKD341. Rockville, MD: Substance Abuse and Mental Health Services Administration, 1999b.

44. http://www.kap.samhsa.gov/products/manuals/index.htm.

45. *Clinical Guidelines for the Use of Buprenorphine in the Treatment of Opioid Addiction.* Treatment Improvement Protocol (TIP) Series 40. DHHS Publication No. (SMA) 04 -3939. Rockville, MD: Substance Abuse and Mental Health Services Administration, 2004. Page 148.

46. Reprinted with written permission from M. Sheehan. Some material from: Center for Substance Abuse Treatment. *Clinical Guidelines for the Use of Buprenorphine in the Treatment of Opioid Addiction.* Treatment Improvement Protocol (TIP) Series 40. DHHS Publication No. (SMA) 04 -3939. Rockville, MD: Substance Abuse and Mental Health Services Administration, 2004. Page 148.

47. Benzodiazepine Task Force on Use, Dependence, Toxicity and Abuse. American Psychiatric Association. 1990.

48. Woods JH, Winger G. Current benzodiazepine issues. *Psychopharmacology.* 1995;118: 107-15.

49. J Pier. Addiction to benzodiazepines – how common? *Arch Fam Med.* 1995;4: 964-70.

50. http://www.benzodiazepine.org/ProfAshtonSymptoms.html

51. http://www.schizophrenia.com/sznews/archives/002223.html

52. Center for Substance Abuse Treatment. *Clinical Guidelines for the Use of Buprenorphine in the Treatment of Opioid Addiction.* Treatment Improvement Protocol (TIP) Series 40. DHHS Publication No. (SMA) 04 -3939. Rockville, MD: Substance Abuse and Mental Health Services Administration, 2004. Page 149-152.

53. http://www.rxlist.com/cgi/generic3/suboxone_wcp.htm

Bibliography

Mahoney D. Dual concerns may hinder buprenorphine Tx. *Clinical Psychiatry News.* 2005; 33:47.

Merrick M. Prescribing buprenorphine: my story. *Internal Medicine News.* 2005; 38:8

Reznik V. Heroin Detoxification with a single high dose of buprenorphine. *The Israel Journal of Psychiatry and Related Sciences.* 2002; 39:113.

Walsh SL, June HL, Schuh KJ, Preston KL, Bigelow GE and Stitzer ML. Effects of buprenorphine and methadone in methadone maintained subjects. *Psychopharmacol.* 1995; 119:268-276.

Walsh SL, Kenzie PL, Stitzer ML, Cone EJ and Bigelow GE. *Clinical Pharmacol Ther.* 1994; 55:569-580.

Wang RIH, Wiesen RL, Lamid S, Roh BL. Rating the presence and severity of opiate dependence. *Clin Pharmacol Ther.* 1974;16:653-658.

The medical ideas, health thoughts, health comments, products and any claims made about specific illnesses, diseases, and causes of health problems in this book, have not been evaluated by the FDA, the USDA, OSHA, CDC, NIH, NIMH or the AMA. Never assume any United States medical body or society, or the majority of American physicians endorse any comment in this book. No comments in this book are approved by any government agency or medical body or society to diagnose, treat, cure or prevent disease. The information provided in this book is for informational purposes only and is not intended as a substitute for the advice from your physician or other health care professional. This book is not intended to replace or adjust any information contained on or in any product label or packaging. You should not use the information in this book for diagnosis or treatment of any health problem or for prescription of any medication or other treatment. You should consult with a healthcare professional before deciding on any diagnosis, or initiating any treatment plan of any kind. Please do not start any diet, exercise or supplementation program, or take any type of nutrient, herb, or medication without clear consultation with your licensed health care provider. If you have or suspect you might have a health problem, please do not use this book to replace a prompt consultation with your health care provider(s).